Born into Violence

Children in the Shadows

Inger Hermann

scm press

Translated by John Bowden from the German '*Halt's Maul, jetzt kommt der Segen . . .' Kinder auf der Schattenseite des Lebens fragen nach Gott*, published 1999 by Calwer Verlag, Stuttgart.

0 334 02817 5

This edition first published 2000 by
SCM Press
9-17 St Albans Place London N1 0NX

SCM Press is a division of
SCM-Canterbury Press Ltd

Printed in Great Britain by
Biddles Ltd, Guildford and King's Lynn

For Almuth-Liesabell

The fact that for seven years I usually taught classes at every level in three Stuttgart schools guarantees the anonymity of the children.

Almost all groups comprised both Catholics and Protestants, boys and girls.

Contents

Introduction

'Our Father, who art in heaven . . .'

'Where's heaven?'

'Heaven? Everywhere. God is everywhere.'

'Is he there among the red lights, then?'

'Red lights? What do you mean?

'You know, where the hookers are. Where the men go to have it off. I just want to know, is God there too?'

And I answer, 'Yes.'

I can speak of God, I can give RE lessons, only because I feel that God is everywhere. The God who is at home in monasteries and churches, to whom I turn in prayer and meditation, whom I can experience under the starry sky – my pupils have never met this God.

There may be varied ways of communicating religious experiences. With these children – children from the big city, uprooted, damaged, humiliated – for me there is only one: to go with them into the depths of their darkest everyday experiences and to trust that, as Paul Tillich says, the name of this unfathomable depth is God.

When a question is asked and with it an abyss is often opened up, I have to be ready to abseil into its darkness. That's what RE means for me.

Sometimes it seems to me that these pupils, even more than their sheltered contemporaries, are interested only in really existential questions. Where is God when someone hits me? Or, Does God like it when my father drinks? Why do we talk about God, if there just isn't a God, can't be a God, in this shitty world?

How can Christ be Lord of those without religion? What does

'religionless Christianity' mean? This question of Bonhoeffer's becomes the central question. We are too little aware that most city children today are 'religionless' in the fullest sense of this word, that they live in a religionless society and grow up to a religionless future. At the same time, whether these children have been baptized or not, it is true of them that 'I have called you by your name. You are mine.' And, amazing though it may sound, this knowledge that they are God's children is not completely submerged; perhaps it is hidden and submerged in the unconscious, but there is a spark which can be kindled.

Many children and young people feel unwanted and superfluous in this world: a burden on parents, neighbours, society. This wound, this sense of not being wanted, cripples their humanity. They feel unsafe, on the dark side of a society which looks away, which doesn't want to feel their needs, their questions and their heartaches. Hilde Domin expresses this well in a poem:

> Your place is where eyes look at you;
> where eyes meet, you come to be . . .
> You fell, but you don't fall,
> Eyes catch you.

For me, that's where RE begins: I catch you by the eyes. I take notice of you. Your truth, not mine, is the starting point.

That this RE, orientated on problems and relationships, easily leads into pastoral care is something that I don't just take into account. I see it as an opportunity.

It means that information about the faith – whether biblical texts, prayers and psalms or church traditions – is not communicated for its own sake, but only to the degree that it becomes transparent to healing experience. It is a waste of time to take children to somewhere that they aren't, outside their anxieties and problems. As long as I leave the often cruel reality of their everyday life outside the school gates, it threatens us like a mad dog. I can tame it only when I have let it into the classroom.

There are two preconditions for healthy RE: the truth of the child and the truthfulness of the teacher. I can endure the often terrifying reality of everyday life only if I meet it with my reality, that means with my whole person. Authenticity is a necessity. Any religious trappings fall away. What is important to me is only what I myself can believe, the experience that is alive in me.

That also means that often I don't have an answer, but communicate to them that I'm not ahead of them in answers, only in the search. If we then succeed in engaging in the search together, because our fear of asking questions gradually dissipates, then RE becomes real and often enjoyable.

Meanwhile I waste no time trying to improve the children's language. The way they talk is hardly prudish. To begin with, their crude language often shocked and hurt me, until I learned that behind the most obscene terms there were either experiences of bitter suffering or deep existential questions. After that I could stop insisting on decent language and by not asking too much of them silence many tormented questions. Now I'm interested only in the outburst, the need that is expressed in it.

That doesn't mean that there are no compulsory forms. I understand them as 'security rituals'. The fixed framework of lessons includes saying a prayer or a psalm together at the beginning and the blessing at the end of the lesson.

Children whose family life is stamped by a random pattern of education and a secularized everyday routine come to sense, for example, that the blessing is not just a set of words, but is really about the presence of God. For seconds, it seems to be a ray of healing in a disquieting abyss of disorientation and a lack of primal trust.

Whereas all children, big and small, usually soon detect that fooling around and disturbances are out of place during blessings and prayers, there is enough room in between for coarseness and fighting, even going so far as verbal and physical violence. This sometimes crude roughness to one another leaves me more at a loss than all the other bits of filth, lesser or greater.

To begin with, I asked myself why these children and young people, who have often been so violated, have no inhibitions at violating one another. Now I know all too well that they hit one another because they themselves are hit. Children who strike one another are children who are struck. In their own suffering they have lost the capacity for compassion. A child whose feelings have been ignored or scorned for years can no longer have any sympathy.

'In every fist there is a whimpering heart.' This sentence can become the key. Can RE change the readiness of children for violence? That is a question which keeps recurring. I am convinced that the problem of the fists can be solved only if we turn to the whimpering hearts. For the sentence can also be reversed: any whimpering heart can become a fist if we do not listen to it.

Can one enter into conversation with these victims of broken relationships, complete drop-outs with a poor vocabulary? Yes, by perceiving their spiritual mutilation. And here the circle closes. If I succeed in also taking note of the violent child respectfully and – if I can summon up the energy – lovingly, amazing things can happen.

I can interrupt fights and try to sort out who is to blame, speak of the virtues of non-violence and fairness – if I am taking on the role of the moral child-tamer. I can also pull away the one who is on top and take him by the arm, stroke his shoulders, his neck or his fist. Often the aggression then immediately and tangibly disappears. With bigger pupils that it is not possible in such an external way, but even with them, by a gentle touch, a question, one can discover, 'What has broken you so, what has hurt you so much that you have to hurt someone else?' As Leo Rosten put it, 'It is the weak who are cruel; one can expect good only of the strong.'

That the Christian churches are facing an uphill struggle, and that the Christianity of the churches is increasingly being detached from social values can be felt in RE as well. The basic conditions – the positioning of the subject in the timetable, the composition of groups, etc. – are one side of the matter. Even more difficult is the devaluation of RE by parents. When a pupil sadly relates that dad says that RE is worthless and hasn't given any money for it, and would give money only for important subjects like maths, then it is clear to me as a teacher that in this subject I, too, have been put on a different scale of values.

I can either lament the increasing secularization, or extend my antennae to detect the longing for religious experience, particularly in this materialistic and consumer-orientated time, a longing which is also increasing. Here I cannot get round the character of RE as 'testimony'. These homeless young people are living in a time of decline, and their anxious anticipation of a threatening future often robs them of the potential to live and learn.

And what do I set against this? A certainty of faith? A canon of values, which after all is fragile enough?

In all the classes we learn Psalm 23: '. . .even if I walk in the darkest valley, I fear no misfortune, for you are with me, your rod and your staff comfort me.' There is no promise here that the dark valley will become light or that one will be taken out of it. 'You are with me.' That is all that I offer them – so to speak as a representative – afresh every lesson: I am ready to go with you into your dark experiences; I will endure the helplessness, even if I cannot help. I will not turn away from the horrible, even if it horrifies me. Alongside your lack of primal trust I will set my trust in your uniqueness and preciousness. Alongside the reality of your despair I will set the reality of God's love. I know that that doesn't explain anything, that it isn't of any use to you – but can you feel that something is changing, in you, in me, in us? I don't even know a name for it. Let's leave it nameless. The unfathomable mystery which does not help and yet changes things. Could the communication of hope look like this?

I hope that theologians will excuse me for often venturing on theologically unsafe ground. There is rarely a possibility to investigate or do research. Theology from the heart may sometimes be open to challenge, but is is more effective and warmer than some assured views of faith.

While I once believed that the way went from the communication of knowledge to upbringing and only exceptionally to relations with the pupils, now I see the pattern of today's RE as moving in the opposite direction: from relationships gradually to upbringing, and then also to the communication of knowledge. Salvation history without healing completely ignores the needs of the children and thus also the needs of school and society.

This RE is a matter of making the holy at home in the coarseness: at Christmas I would say that it is about God's birth in a stable.

There's War in My Country:
Uprooted Children

Moses in the underground garage

Medine is sitting on the floor outside her classroom door. I've a gap between lessons and am rushing to copy something. When I get back, she's still sitting there, in the same position, white-faced, almost rigid. I ask her, 'What's the matter?' Medine, who usually greets me with a wild embrace, remains impassive. I squat down beside her, and am shocked by her expression: hatred, fury and grief are chiselled into a child's face. She shakes off the hand I put on her shoulder. 'Teachers are shit,' she hisses crossly. 'School's shit. Everything's shit.' Medine is a keen little girl, and her pain quite clearly goes deeper than annoyance with the class teacher. 'Was your mum cross with you today?' I ask. Medine nods silently. 'Hit you?' Medine is silent.

Then quietly: 'She hit me and kicked me and pulled my hair and shrieked and shrieked.'

'Why's your mum so cross with you?'

'I don't know. She shrieked that I was a whore.'

I feel a bit queasy. 'And your dad,' I nevertheless ask, 'does he hit you too?' She shakes her head. 'He's always nice to me.'

'And when mum hits you?'

'Then he's already at work.'

The bell goes. RE lesson. Medine immediately goes in with me. Peter and Sabine are also already there. Olli, the baby of the class, comes running in, slams down his schoolbag, goes to the table and like lightning daubs it with wild lines, whorls and arrows. Oh Olli, I think, how can you bear your life, how can you still always laugh, enjoy playing, and sometimes – very rarely – even listen to a story?

A colleague had telephoned me a week earlier, when Olli's mother had died in an alcoholic coma. His father, drunk, fell out of the window and is in hospital with many fractured bones. The same day the four children went into a home.

'Olli's scribbling all over the table,' squeaks Vera in an accusing way, 'Is he allowed to do that?'

By now all eight pupils are up in the RE room.

'It's hot.'

'I don't want RE today.'

'I'm tired.'

'I want a drink.'

'And I'm hungry.'

Lesson six. And it is unbearably hot. How can I arouse even a spark of interest in Moses' fate in these conditions?

'What's up?' I ask. It's now getting on my nerves too.

'I'm so hungry. I haven't had anything to eat.'

It really gets to me. What I would most like to do is to send them all home, but that's not on. Then I remember that I've some bread down below in the car.

A minute later we're creeping downstairs on tiptoe, quiet as mice. I open the door to the garage.

'Don't put on the light, we want to go down in the dark,' says one child.

'All right,' I say. It's two flights of stairs, but they won't fall. It gets darker and darker and wonderfully cool. They are completely silent; two of them have seized my hands. By now it's pitch dark. Suddenly one of them begins to shriek – just like that, nothing has happened – and now they all shriek, shout and yell. It's deafening, a primaeval cry of piercing pain and wild joy. Then I press the switch. Light. They immediately stop. Olli wants to open the heavy door to the parking area.

'Which is your car?' They rush towards it.

Now I could have taken the bread and gone upstairs with it.

But it's cool and quiet here. They're ready to try without pushing and shoving, and all nine of us manage to fit into the car. It's a really tight fit and very cosy. I share out the bread, two slices each. By now the garage light has gone out. This is more than a car in the underground garage; it's the safe, primaeval cave. And something else is satisfied as well as the lunchtime hunger.

There's just one more slice of bread for each child. Today I had wanted to tell them about Moses, about his mother's distress at Pharaoh's order to kill the children, about the care with which she launched him on the river in a basket, about this perilous childhood which was at the same time guarded by God himself. So that's what I begin to tell them in the dark, almost whispering – and they listen, excited and attentive as never before all that year. I get to the end. 'Right, now we're going back up; you can take your schoolbags and go home.'

'And the blessing?' asks Tonio.

'You're right.' They fold their hands: 'God, bless us and protect us . . . and give us your peace.'

They squeeze out of the car and rush over the parking area. My God, I think, at last a good RE lesson. You've given us your peace, thank you.

'Don't put on the light.' They want to go up the stairs in the dark again. Because of me. Laughter and shrieking. Then the light goes on and in a second they fall on Diego, slapping him, kicking him, punching him. He put the light on. Now he's lying on the floor, wide-eyed with terror: 'Coward, spoilsport.' They kick him. I leap up the stairs, and push them all to one side. 'Stop!' 'He's scared, he's a coward. Scared of the dark. What a baby!' Yelling and mocking. Now I'm furious and hurt. This horde of little beasts! What have they done to the peace which we just had and which so refreshed me for a while?

I pick up Diego from the ground. He hasn't been with us long. His drawing is extraordinarily gifted, but sometimes I find his silences almost uncanny.

'Diego isn't cowardly, he's sensible. He knows that bad things can happen in the dark,' I thunder at the children, without reflecting on whether what I say makes sense. His nose is bleeding, and I hold my handkerchief to it. We go upstairs in front of the others.

'Tell me, Diego, what bad things happen when it's dark?' I ask him.

'In the night – men come – they kill people – sometimes even children.' He stutters. Diego comes from Latin America. Is there something about that in his records?

Inside school we meet the headmaster. 'Where have you come from?' he asks. 'RE in the garage?'

'Yes, brilliant,' says Melanie.

'And what did you learn there?' he asks her.

'That the wicked king Pharaoh couldn't bear foreigners either. Just because Moses is not his people. He even killed the foreigners!'

Tonio is certainly one of the brightest children in the class. I had said nothing about foreigners, but Tonio clearly already knows the meaning of xenophobia well enough.

They've all got their bags and have gone home. I can go too. I'm exhausted. When will I learn that success doesn't last and cannot be hoarded like a treasure? We experienced security and peace in the car in the underground garage – does it stop being a healing experience because everyday life hits back at us with violence and fear? And the bad experience when the little beasts set on Diego – is it only bad? Wasn't he able to speak of his anxiety for the first time?

Our assessment of RE with these children – good and bad, healthy and unhealthy – is providing completely new answers. A different one every lesson. I think of some lines by Rilke:

'People keep looking away from God. They seek him in the light . . ., above. – And God waits elsewhere – waits – at the very ground of all things. Deep. Where there are roots. Where it is warm and dark.' Did Rilke know the underground garage?

Humans can do everything: shit and love

Today it's sports day. In the RE lesson I have only the three who aren't taking part. We're still getting the chairs away from the desks when Sven shoots in. He drops his sports bag and his helmet by the door.

'Frau Hermann, could you quickly say the blessing?'

'I thought that you were involved in sports day.'

'Yes, but surely a blessing can't hurt?'

Before the amen is finished he picks up his things and rushes after the others.

Fat Otto shakes his head at so much hectic activity. He takes another bite from the roll under his desk and asks – bulging cheeks, but with the eyes of a wise man:

'Is praying and all that any use?'

We reflect. Can people influence God? Doesn't God do what he wants anyway?

'I believe that the devil does what he wants and God can't do anything anyway. You can see that on the TV,' says Dragomir, a passionate Croat.

'And if people do such devilish stuff, kill others and all that – I mean criminals and such people – does God still love the criminals?' Mario wants to know.

Otto, 'Of course, they're God's children.'

Mario, 'Even when they do shit?'

Otto, chewing, 'My mother loves me even when I do shit.'

Mario, 'Idiot, God isn't your mother.'

Dragomir, 'Then my father. My father hits me sometimes, but he still loves me. He said he would visit me even in prison.'

By now Otto has munched through his roll – though I haven't of course been able to see behind the hands he is holding in front of himself.

'Wait a minute, I think that God loves me, whether or not I do shit, because God can't do anything but love. Isn't that right? Only we humans can do lots of other things, kill and so on.' Otto breaks off and sinks into philosophical reflection.

Dragomir (top of the class – why is he in this school?) sums up:

'The devil can do shit, God can only love, and only humans can do everything: shit and love.'

And some people still say that remedial pupils are dim.

We aren't really a school for the stupid

Great confusion. The class teacher is still visibly exhausted by her own row, the reverberations of which could be heard down the corridor.

'Good luck with the mob,' she wishes me with a tired smile. This morning the police had been there: Robbi had been firing shots with a gas pistol and two pupils are in hospital.

I would rather have gone out in a tropical storm than entered this turbulent classroom. (And I still hardly know the pupils' names.)

Veronica waves a black book around.

'Do you want to see it? My language and your language in one book. All about God in both languages.'

Her priest in Stuttgart has given her a little book with the Catholic mass and some texts and hymns: Italian on the left, German on the right.

'Read something to us.'

By chance I hit on the ten commandments. Veronica, usually somewhat faltering in expression, chatters on like a sewing machine. The other pupils turn round in amazement. 'What's going on?'

It's worth making use of the calm.

'Write a commandment on the board. The fifth . . .' (because linguistically it's the simplest).

Veronica writes. 'Non uccidere.'

'I know that in Spanish,' says Maria. 'No mates.'

'And I know it in Yugoslavian.' 'Ti nesmies ubiti.'

'That's Croatian,' says Alex. 'May I write it in Slovenian?'

'And I in Polish!' Milena comes to the front.

Down at the bottom there is still room for 'Do not kill' and at the top for 'Du sollst nicht töten.'

We count: seven languages.

'We really aren't a school for the stupid if we can write down the fifth commandment in so many languages,' remarks Jochen (whose dearest wish is to get back to ordinary school).

I think that too.

Keenly and peacefully they copy what they have put together on the board into their books. And in that way order came out of chaos.

'Shut up, it's time for the blessing'

Trees quite clearly aren't there to grow up to heaven.

I go into the classroom still having a good feeling from the last lesson. (Though somewhat flustered and almost ten minutes late because of a traffic jam. This driving between schools wears me down.)

It's Veronica again.

'Come and see what's in this cupboard.'

She's taken out a thick roll of paper and unrolls it on the floor: around twelve almost life-size photographs depict human development from the baby to the adult, naked of course, male and female. In a flash almost everyone has picked up a poster and now it starts.

'That's Patrick – You idiot, he's got a much bigger one – Halil in Class 9. You should see that Georgia . . .'

They're so excited. They use such coarse language, with a vocabulary previously unknown to me – it's like a jungle and a forest fire simultaneously. I really can't take it: my back hurts, my heart races. 'Impulse to flee' is a tame word for my need; I just have to get away from these children. I sit on my chair and do nothing. After a while they notice that I'm not doing anything. Paula asks in amazement,

'Don't you think that these are revolting?'

'No,' I say, and because there's something approaching silence, I add without thinking. 'All right, now put them in order of size.'

They are so amazed that immediately they begin to push benches aside, pile up chairs, to make room for the gallery of nudes.

There's a knock. A colleague looks in, 'Sorry to disturb you' – a baffled look. 'Anything's possible in RE,' she seems to think, and leaves us again. It's almost time for the closing blessing – which, as they know by now, they will not be spared. The twelve nudes are rolled up again and put in the cupboard. A kind of peaceful state of exhaustion prevails in the class.

Veronica speaks out: 'Probably the class teacher wants to give us some enlightenment with the posters. But really we don't need it. I think we could teach you something. Don't you?'

Certainly, I'm convinced of that. The bell goes. Gianni turns to Veronica.

'Shut up, it's time for the blessing. I want to go to break.' All join in saying, 'The Lord bless us and protect us . . . and give us his peace.'

Good girls and condoms

Daniela (twelve) and Kerstin (thirteen) are panting from fighting each other when I come in. When she sees me, Melanie jumps up and shouts,

'Just look at what that pig has in her bag.'

'What have you got in your bag, Daniela?'

'Condoms,' she says defiantly, 'but that's not filthy, is it?'

'No, not if you need them. But why do you need them?'

'I'm having a competition with a friend to see who collects the most. I've already got twenty-five.'

'And where do you get them from?'

'These? Oh, from my brother.'

'Liar, liar,' shouts Melanie. 'You don't have a brother.'

'I meant to say my father,' Daniela defends herself. 'Sometimes I also buy some. Do you want to see them, Frau Hermann? They smell really good. Sometimes of chocolate or lemon.'

'Have you opened them, then?'

'No, you can smell them through the paper.'

She promptly holds a handful under my nose – but I think that it's time to begin the lesson.

We pray, 'By good powers wonderfully protected, confident we wait for come what may . . .'

Dragomir interrupts the amen.

'Why can't we say a proper prayer, about God or Mary – something more holy?'

'Why isn't that a proper prayer?' I ask in amazement.

It proves that Dragomir has misheard: with the alteration of two words in German, 'By good powers wonderfully protected' becomes 'From good girls wonderfully born'.

'We never said comic prayers like that in Sarajevo!'

I believe in God only in Portugal

Paula is really having a bad time. Sometimes she dozes in a miserable way, and when I try to get her to take her book out or to read a sentence, the big girl becomes as stubborn as a three-year-old. She won't, she can't, no – and anyway . . .

Then, suddenly, a flood of tears.

To begin with that frightened me. What was it that was so bad? I sat on her desk, put my hand on her shoulder and simply went on teaching – while she went on sobbing under me, almost comfortably. It took me a while to recognize the pattern, stubbornness – weeping – comfort, and also that Paula seemed almost set on it. All right, I would stop playing along with her.

So I stopped asking anything of her, and ignored her refusals. It went on like that for two or three lessons. Suddenly the chair next to her fell on the floor. In the next lesson a book hit the door. 'Are you out of your mind?', I asked her, and she promptly burst into tears. She had me where she wanted me.

'Oh, just let her go on blubbering,' advise her fellow pupils. 'Paula's just a cry-baby.' They're probably right.

Nevertheless I want to try something else. Paula clearly depends on my gestures of comfort. What if I were now to 'comfort' her before the outburst?

'Comfort food', I tell myself, and write it in red in my preparation book.

I look out for her before the lesson, ask her to help with the books, admire her hairstyle, and when telling a story put myself almost within touching distance beside her, say good-bye after every lesson with a handshake – and all the stubbornness, all the babyish crying, is wiped away.

That sounds like a success story, but in fact it is merely the prelude to a very sad story.

Paula now often goes with me to the school gate. On one occasion she pushes her thick black hair aside so that I can see the dark red scratch-marks on her neck; on another occasion she lifts up her T-shirt: long, bluish-green weals.

'Mum simply hates me – she hits me every day. And I hate her.'

I go to the headmaster, to the liaison teacher. What can we do? Someone from the social services has already been there. I talk with Paula. She's terrified. 'Don't send anyone! Please don't send anyone! That makes it all worse! The last time a woman from the social services came, mum spoke with a comic high voice, and almost before the woman got to the bottom of the stairs she hit me harder than ever. I thought she wanted to kill me.'

But it can't go on like this. Nor does it. Paula runs off to her divorced father. For two weeks she comes to school punctually and doesn't stare in front of her in such a glazed way. Then her mother gets her back.

It's the first lesson on Wednesday, and under the hearing 'God says Yes to me' we pray a modern version of Psalm 139: 'Lord, you see through me, you know me through and through . . .' Paula arrives, twenty minutes late, slumps into her place, puts her head on the desk. The discussion goes on.

'Does God say yes to everyone? When babies are baptized – the pastor said that this is God's yes. Is that right?'

'It's all rubbish. There isn't a God. Enough of that,' Paula hisses furiously.

'I think Paula's right,' says Fabio. 'I don't believe in God either.'

'Nor do I, nor do I,' I hear from various pupils.

Interest in God's yes has turned into a sorrowful-defiant no to God.

Paula has sat down, her chin in her hands. She's an attractive girl with those big dark eyes and that full black hair, but her hopelessness makes her seem old, almost weary of life.

'It's like this. In Portugal I believe in God. But in Germany – I can't believe in God in Germany.'

Then she tells how she came to Germany when she was three years old. Before that she lived with her grandmother in Portugal. Her grandmother often told her about God, took her to church and – 'grandma was always kind'. Then her mother took her away. 'She doesn't want to talk about God or pray; she certainly doesn't do that. It isn't like her or like Germany and so I don't believe in God in Germany.'

Yesterday was the last day of school before the summer holidays. My study is filled with the scent of a single rose, a big glorious flower with a short stem. Paula gave it to me as we said good-bye. For the holidays she's going to Portugal – perhaps she'll be allowed to stay with grandma. 'With grandma and God,' I say. We both laugh.

'Tell me, 'I ask her, 'where did you get this beautiful rose?' 'Oh,' she says, does that really matter?'

'Yes, Paula, it does matter. Thank you for the rose.'

She comes with me to the school gate as often in the last year.

How good it would be if Paula could stay in her country, where alienation, despair, hatred and beatings do not make any experience of God impossible for her.

'I believe I God only in Portugal,' she said.

The rose smells fragrant – even pilfered roses smell fragrant, I think; and I'm glad.

I've never loved anyone as much as my rabbit

Things are going from bad to worse with Marion. By now one's got used to her late arrivals every day and her refusal to join in the lesson. 'But now that she's also beginning to steal, there must be an end to it.' My colleague is clearly exhausted, overwhelmed by the magnitude of the problems.

Marion hasn't gone out at break time; she hangs around the

classroom. She isn't attractive, she isn't clever or diligent or tidy. Nevertheless I like her. So I adopt the direct approach.

'Tell me, what's all this about stealing?'

She blushes to the roots of her hair, and bows her head in silence.

'You need money. But do you need so much money?'

'Yes,' she breathes, 'it's because of my rabbit.'

'Because of your rabbit?'

'Yes, my rabbit. He's the only friend I have. I've never loved anyone as much as my rabbit. I'm worried that when he dies I won't have anyone else; then I'll die too.'

'Why do you think that your rabbit could die?'

'Because he keeps squeaking and won't eat. My cousin trod on him.'

'Trod on the rabbit.'

'And threw him across the kitchen by his ears. I shrieked, but then he threw him again. As a punishment.'

'A punishment? For what?'

'Because – because I wanted to stop sleeping with him.'

'Stop sleeping with him?' Marion is fourteen.

'Yes, because there's war in our country. So my cousin has come to Germany. And my father said he had to sleep in my room, because we have only two rooms. And that's how it started.'

'And now you want to stop?'

'I don't know. But when my mother got to hear about it she half killed me. She says that she'll kill me if I get pregnant. That's why. And now Drago is tormenting my rabbit.'

'And that's what you need money for?'

'Yes, because the vet costs fifty marks. And the rabbit is in such a bad state. His ear is all bloody.'

She begins to cry. The bell rings. End of break.

'But don't tell anyone. I must rush to the toilet.'

Her tearstained face can do with a wash. Nevertheless I hold her back.

'Will you tell me the name of your vet? Then I'll telephone him. Then you can take the rabbit without paying.'

'Really? Do you think that will work?'

'Yes, and then you won't have to steal.'

'No. Why else?'

She stands there as if bathed in light. Her snotty face, her shaggy hair, her crumpled T-shirt. She really is an attractive girl – why did I never see that?

'Marion seems to have made a new start,' my colleague remarks a few days later. I also get that expression.

Then the rabbit dies. Despite the vet. And it begins all over again.

Looking for God in the depths – how often do I think or say that sentence to myself? But what if depth follows depths? If depths are so deep that there is hardly any light and air left to breathe for a child like Marion? I've no objection to continuing to go with her into the depths, the dirty, mean, hopeless areas of her life, but what if God is not to be found there? If the hem of his garment, the breath of his presence evades us, to leave us even more helpless?

I quarrel with this God, who cannot save even a rabbit.

Corpses in the river – that's better

He's a head taller than all the others in Class 4 and always engaged in using his fists or – with a supreme effort of will – not using them for a few minutes.

No one knows how old he really is. Santos from Mozambique. When talking to adults he prefers to keep his hands, like dangerous instruments, in his pockets. He stands there like a young bull, ready for the attack.

At first I thought that he was unteachable, but I soon found out that there were two situations which really soaked up his wild aggression. Exciting, tense story-telling – including biblical stories – and vivid pictures of danger and spiritual distress utterly absorb him. Then his eyes – in which the white of the pupil contrasts almost unnaturally with his very dark skin – are big and attentively directed forward; his shoulders and hands are relaxed, neither in action nor in his trouser pockets. It's the same with painting and drawing. Then he can erupt in an intoxication with colours: wild and bizarre forms, radiant pictures.

Woe to anyone who disturbs Santos then! If disturbed, in seconds he unleashes his concentrated energy on the person concerned. A punch in the mouth or the face or a kick on the shin are the least reactions.

The story of Moses in Egypt offers enough violence and torment to absorb Santos.

'Egypt is in Africa?' Usually he rarely speaks or asks questions.

'Yes, Egypt is also Africa, in the north; Mozambique is more in the south.'

'Go on,' is all he says.

The ten plagues which the Lord sends on Pharaoh's people fascinates Santos. Plagues of locusts, swarms of mosquitoes, dying cattle – he knows all that from his Africa. Bloody river water. There's something breathless in his attention.

'But how can a river have bloody water?', Kathrin wonders.

'Shut your mouth,' snarls Santos.

'But that doesn't happen,' she insists.

'Damn it. Of course it does. You just need to get rid of enough corpses.'

'Get rid of what?'

'Corpses, stupid. Go on with the story!'

'Tell me, Santos,' I ask, 'have you seen that on TV or for real?'

'For real. In my country there's war. Usually. Anyway, the river is better than burning.'

'Why?'

'Burning stinks so much and it takes a long time. But now go on with the story of Moses.'

I try, but I can't continue. They can paint.

At last the lesson comes to an end.

'This is for you.' Santos holds up his picture in front of me, an orgy in black and red.

'Do you think of this often?', I ask him.

'Sometimes. My uncle's arm didn't burn. I went back the next day. It was still there. Then I ran away.'

'And now you're with your parents and your sister in Germany?'

'They aren't my parents and Maria isn't my sister. They took me with them.'

'And your parents?'

'Don't know. No one knows. There's a war on at home.'

He picks up his school bag and knocks over a chair without noticing it. I say nothing.

'Bye till next week.'

'Bye.'

'Will you go on with the story?'

'Yes, I'll go on. And thanks for the picture.'

Monk in battledress

A lesson on the Bible, its history, its structure.

Bernd is being stubborn again: 'It's idiotic: "Book of Books". That's the last book I'd read.'

The others are attentively copying the first sentence of the Old Testament in Hebrew script from the blackboard: 'In the beginning, God . . .'

Then the last sentence in the New Testament in Greek characters.

Berndt goes on objecting: 'I just don't want to copy down those stupid squiggles.'

'What do you want to do?'

'Drive a tank. Flatten Chetniks.'

'Do you think that will achieve anything?'

'Don't know. But it would be fun.'

He looks at me in a challenging way. Clearly he wants another power struggle. I don't. But how can I get round it? The camouflage suit which he often wears already unnerves me.

Nora pipes up. She's a big, temperamental gypsy girl with wild hair. Although colleagues describe her as coarse and violent, I like her character.

'You once said that the strong should help the weak. Is that right?'

'That's right.'

'I'm stronger than Bernd. I beat him yesterday.'

'Did you? So what next?'

I turn round and again write on the board:

The grace of the Lord be with you all . . .

Grace to and fro. It's enough for me. This constant struggle against apathy and crudeness. I draw a parchment scroll, the original form of the holy book. Then Norah taps me on the shoulder and holds out two books, hers and Bernd's, and says in the broadest Swabian: 'There are your holy worms. I've drawn them. And now you needn't quarrel with Bernd!'

'And why shouldn't I quarrel with Bernd?'

'Because it doesn't suit you!'

Bernd grins contentedly.

Next lesson. All the pupils have baked cakes in the cooking lesson. They can take their giant confections home. The whole room smells of honey and spices.

So I tell them how these Christmas cakes originated in the monasteries; how honey was so to speak a by-product of making candles, and the spices first of all came from the East as a medicine. The Crusaders may have played a role here.

'Crusaders?' Bernd's ears prick up. 'Who were they? You can certainly tell us more about them.'

I talk about the Crusades.

When the bell rings, he is nevertheless once again first to the door. No one gets out as quickly as Bernd. Suddenly he comes back, breaks his cake down the middle and offers me half. 'There, for you.'

'For me? Don't you want to take it home?'

'Yes, but I can bake more. I can do that as well as your monks!'

Bernd, my monk in battledress.

Does your God really know foreigners too?

Mirella look pale and is crying.

'If my mother also loses her job, we'll have to go back. What would we live on here? Praying's no use.'

'And you don't want to go back to Slovenia?'

'What would I do there? I don't know my way around there. After all, I was born here. What are foreigners anyway? In Slovenia they laugh as soon as I open my mouth.'

Tears run down her face.

There's nothing comforting to say.

Suddenly she throws her head back and snaps at me, 'Does your God really know foreigners too?'

Other pupils come up and interrupt us – but in any case I didn't have an answer to her question.

We keep working on the subject of yesterday's lesson, 'Humans ask about God'. For most pupils it's boring. Only Mirella is utterly caught up in it.

'I wish that there was a God, but there isn't. Unfortunately.'

'How do you know that so clearly?', I ask.

'From the devil, who I believe in. I can't do otherwise. I just know that the devil exists – he's in me, in my dreams, in my anxiety, everywhere. But God – I don't know where God is.'

Mirella, two weeks later. When asked about her greatest hope, her dearest wish, she replies: 'For my mother to cook again as before.'

'Doesn't she cook any more?'

Mirella replies hesitantly, as though she were spelling through a difficult text.

'Since father lost his job – quite a long time ago now – mother has gone out to clean – in a canteen. Yes, father is mostly at home. – What does he do? Drink, of course. What else? – I don't like going home after school any more. Before, it used to smell of food at lunchtime, but now it smells of beer and cigarettes. When mother comes home she's done in. Sometimes she brings remnants from the canteen, but the food's so cold and slimy that I don't like it. Then she gives me two or three marks, with which I buy myself something sweet.'

The pretty and lively girl of last year has become lethargic and bad-tempered.

Her greatest hope, that her mother has done some cooking

again when she gets in – she cannot believe in the God who
cannot fulfil this for her.

Happiness? That's not on

'Everyone wants to be happy' runs the heading in the book.
   'That's true,' thinks Fred, 'I'm happy anyway.'
   'My sister is happy, but I'm happy only sometimes,' says Peter.
   'What about you?,' I turn to the silent Dragana.
   'Me? Happiness? That's not on.'
   It sounds so dark, so final, that any encouraging remark seems
to me to be shallow.
   The discussion goes on. Then I give out sheets on which they're
to write what is important for them.
   'Can we also draw?' asks Dragana.
   'Yes, you can also draw. Do you want coloured pencils?'
   'Don't need them. Black's enough!'
   They're all busy. The drawing was a good idea. Then they
needn't torment themselves with the German language and the
difficult orthography.
   Dragana came with her mother from Croatia two or three
years previously. They live in a tiny one-and-a-half room apart-
ment on a noisy street. She's an attractive girl, but seems to be
turned in on herself, bowed down under a heavy burden.
   I collect the sheets. The children go off for break. Dragana's
sheet is on top. She's at the door when I call her back.
   'Can you tell me something about your picture?'
   She sucks in her cheeks.
   'A big house. I wish we had a big house with a garden round
it.'
   'Yes, your house is splendid, all those windows and the hand-
some entrance. But it looks as if no one is living there.'
   'No one is. The grown-ups have all gone to war.'
   'But there are lots of children in the garden.'
   'Yes. All the children are playing in the garden.'
   'And what are they playing?'
   'War, of course.'

'Why are they playing war?'

'Because, on the left, those are the children of Serbs; there are more of them and on the other side are our children. We are fewer, and we don't have as many weapons as the Chetniks.'

'You call them Chetniks?'

'We didn't use to, when we still played properly. Then we always said their name. But then they mocked us and called us Ustasha. That's why.'

'What about you? Are you also in the picture?'

'Yes and no. You can't see me – because I've hidden in the cellar.'

'In the cellar?'

She nods.

'Because I'm always afraid.'

'And do you feel safe in the cellar?'

'No, the house gets blown up anyway.'

She points to the rockets which are falling on the house. One has gone through the roof.

'And the blue flashes and all those thin blue threads which reach everywhere, even as far as the children?'

'They're dangerous rays.'

'Dangerous rays? What are they?'

'I don't quite know. Except that it's dangerous. Because of war and anxiety – and everyone hates one another.'

'Do you sometimes talk about this with your mother?'

'No. Then she only cries. In any case because of dad. Perhaps he's already dead. She keeps hearing news from Croatia.'

'And what else does she do?'

'Nothing. She just sits there gawking. Always at one place. She doesn't say anything. Almost nothing. She wants to go home, even though there's a war on.'

'What about you? Do you want to go back too?'

'I'm scared.'

'Are you scared all the time?'

'Not always. Not when I'm at school. That's why I like being here at school best.'

The guitar and the little scapegoat

'Today you've got it easy,' the secretary says as I arrive, 'only three scapegoats from Class 4. They aren't allowed to go to the National Youth Games.'

The three 'goats' sit on the tables and listlessly dangle their legs.

'We don't want RE today,' they grumble at me.

I can understand that in their situation.

'All right, let's play a game.'

'Games are boring. Not a game.'

'Then I'll tell you about a captured chamois in Africa.'

'Why should I want to know about a chamois? I'm not interested in Africa.'

'What are you interested in, then, Peter?'

'Me? Oh, nothing.'

'What would you like to do best if school was over?'

'Nothing in particular. Watch a video.'

'And when you're grown-up – if you were granted a wish, what would you wish then?'

'To be a gangster and make everyone afraid of me. The Chetniks most of all.'

His little eyes look at me full of hatred. What have those child's eyes already seen, what has this soul and puny little body already seen in nine years?

'Do you know what . . .', I begin, and put my hand on his shoulder.

'Don't touch me!' he snorts, and jumps from the table.

There's a guitar in the corner. He picks it up and plucks the strings roughly and wildly.

'Give it to me, I'll tune it for you, then it won't sound so terrible.'

We now sit side by side on the floor, almost in harmony.

'Do you know the names of the strings?' I ask while tuning it.

'Couldn't care less.'

'Eat A Donkey, Go Home Early.'

'What on earth are you talking about?'

'About eating a donkey.'

'But that's rubbish!'

'But it's practical rubbish. It helps you to remember which string is which.'

'Can I have it now?'

Peter again puts the guitar on his lap. The strumming already sounds better. Now he plucks individual strings, concentrating hard.

Juan and Marcus scribble filth on the table with equal concentration. At last they're undisturbed: they have the whole table and all the colours. Painful, infuriating, I would have thought until recently. Splendid, I think today; they should do it more often.

I remain sitting on the floor beside Peter. His fidgets, his poisonous irritability have disappeared. With concentration he looks for individual notes.

'Why don't we learn the guitar?' It sounds almost a plea.

'If you want to play the guitar so much, perhaps you can get your parents . . .'

'Don't have any.'

'What don't you have?'

'Parents.'

'Oh, you no longer have a dad.'

'Never had one, because he's a pig.'

'I say nothing. Touch the bunches of strings which he's striking. It sounds almost beautiful.

'Damned Chetniks.' Peter hurls the guitar away.

'Chetniks? Who?'

'My dad. Serbian pigs. It's his fault that my granddad – they killed him.'

'Who says that?'

'My mum. We're Croatians. When I'm sixteen I'll beat it and kill them all.'

'Who?'

'The Serbian pigs of course!'

'But your father . . .'

'He isn't my father! He's a Chetnik!'

His eyes are slits. Hatred. Or longing? Both: 'Hatred is hungry love.' I've never seen that more clearly.

'The bell will go soon. Now we must say the blessing,' calls out Juan.

'I don't need a shit blessing,' shouts Peter. He gives the guitar a kick and rushes out of the classroom. Juan and Marcus look questioningly at me.

'Come on, let's say the blessing for Peter too.'

'Should we still bless someone who behaves like an arsehole?' Marcus is indignant.

'Because he's sad, because he's had more than anyone can take, yes we should.'

'I don't think so.'

God, bless us and protect us . . . and give us your peace.

Reflections

The beginning of the school year. I'm giving out coloured sheets for the children to write their names on, and also to write something that they like to do.

Petra, babysitting; Giovanni, football, I read. And then on a sheet, in capitals: 'People don't know me. What do I like to do? Nothing.'

'That's probably Dragomir, who's so pale and puny. He hasn't been in Germany very long,' a colleague explains later.

In the next lesson I greet him: 'Hello, Dragomir.' He turns his head away. 'Isn't that your name?'

'No it's not.'

'What do your parents call you them?'

'They don't.'

'And when your father calls you?'

'He doesn't. He's dead.'

Later I learn that his father is dead, his grandfather, his big brother – all are dead. For a brief year he has been living in Germany with his mother and little sister.

The real losers in wars are the children, because what usually cannot be built up again in them – trust in grown-ups – has been destroyed.

The experiences and impressions of war, the feeling of being homeless in a threatening world, makes their soul a wasteland on which nothing will grow any more. These are children who wither before they blossom.

A study of pupils who are weak at school comes to the result that in 42.9% of cases the impact on behaviour at school and psychology is directly connected with serious conflict situations and a major change in environment.

A change of environment: memories of home are overlaid with images of terrifying and inhuman events. A world in which friends can become enemies, relatives can become traitors and neighbours murderers – in such a world there is nothing to laugh at and nothing to hope for. A destroyed childhood, a plundered future.

The catastrophe of psychological disturbance and a complete loss of orientation provides the breeding-ground for dull hatred: depending on the situation, hatred of life becomes hatred of the neighbour, hatred of the world in general. And do we still wonder at their potential for aggression, the apparently cold-blooded way in which they torment others? The aggressive child is often desperate. Is this violence an attempt to cope with terrifying reality? Children's violence is often inseparable from adult violence.

This violence is not always directed outwards. The experience of homelessness and a void in life can equally be expressed in a complete lack of interest, a depressive shunning of contacts and thoughts of suicide.

A twelve-year-old identifies with Anne Frank. 'I like her because she's in such despair. She seems like me. She's very sad because she has no home and is afraid of all that's coming. And she's right: she didn't have a future because they killed her.' That means: I don't have a future any more, because they've killed my trust, my love, my hope. So these children are sitting in front of me and I want to do RE. Religion – *religio*, the bond with a divinity, the good, the holy? Sometimes I'm really glad that the Bible doesn't just contain 'holy' writings but fratricide, betrayal, slavery, war, fear and death.

The children are interested in these stories; they discover themselves in this hopeless distress. But isn't there a way out for them somewhere? Grace, love, redemption? Don't they need that above all? That could be – but I don't have it. I don't have it there to give, as I can give a bit of bread, an apple, a coin.

Does that mean that everything remains as it is and they stay in their prison of fear and loneliness? If I succeed in opening the door to their dark dungeon a little, so that they begin to talk about their bad experiences, a process can begin. I have often asked myself how it is that healing forces are released in talking about suffering.

Conversations against fear? Fear constricts us, makes us unable to

breathe. The experience of fear becomes an experience of imprison-
ment: constraint, cold, loneliness, darkness. Life goes rigid. But we need
breath to speak. In many peoples and religions breath is the real princi-
ple of life. In Genesis we read: 'Then God made the man from a lump of
earth and breathed into him a living breath. So the man became a living
being' (2.7).

In speech, breath moves, the constriction of the chest is relieved and
breath streams through us. The breath of God? The child sitting there,
huddled up like a dark clod of earth, changes into a living being.
Talking with someone is talking with God. Accepting the fear. It is
suppressed fear, fear that is pushed away, that takes its revenge on life.

Sometime it all begins with a biblical story. The Israelites' fear of the
violent Pharaoh, Jacob's homelessness when fleeing from his brothers –
and then a child says, 'I know that. When we left home . . .'

Sometimes it also begins with a memory: 'My uncle, that's dad's
brother, betrayed us, because . . .', and then we think of the brothers
who sold little Joseph abroad.

There is no story which gets to them simply through the content communicated in the words. It is always important for us also to share our
feelings as we listen, reflect and talk together. And every feeling may be
there, including hatred and rage, disgust and pain. Again it's a matter
of paying attention to the child's fate, of getting to know children
cautiously.

'People don't know me,' wrote Dragomir. If the answer to the
question 'Who are you?' is 'I am not', then it is a matter of re-creation,
rediscovery. If you are not, if people don't know you, than I will now go
in search of you, find you, get to know you.

Here the boundary between education and therapy has been crossed,
but I am certain that only value-free care can – perhaps – prevent the
homeless from becoming warriors, the victims from becoming per-
petrators.

Ways out of fear? I know that I can't make a promising sprinter out
of someone with one leg, but I can encourage him to hop. No more.

2

Maltreated and Abused

God's certainly cross with me

Alex is a handsome boy, tall and slim, with his brown complexion, his well-proportioned features, his unruly hair. But his look! Often he narrows his big dark eyes – is it anxiety or rage, sorrow?

Now he's standing in front of me, the tall boy, somewhat intimidated and shy.

'I'm really a Catholic,' he begins.

'Yes, I know. But it doesn't matter, feel free . . .'

'No, I mean, I've heard that if you're a Catholic you can go to a priest and tell him everything. Even bad things, crap and so on. And then he somehow puts it right again. Is that true?'

'You mean go to confession.'

'Precisely. That's the word, confess. But if you don't know a priest. And you're afraid. I mean, in that case can you . . .? I mean a teacher . . .? You know what I mean.'

'You're wondering whether you can tell me what's bothering you?'

'Yes, and whether that will then put everything right.'

'Alex, we can talk about it, about the bad thing. But I just don't know whether that will put everything right.'

'But at least you can pray.'

'So can you.'

'I don't know God very well, and besides, I always think that now he's certainly cross with me.'

'Alex must come to the gym,' shouts a fellow pupil up the stairs.

'Look,' I ask him, 'would you like to come to me sometime and then we'll have more time to talk about?'

'Yes – No . . .' He bows his head and blushes deeply.

'No, I'd rather not come. Not talk. They're such difficult things, the crap and so on . . . Can I write it down?'

'You can also write it down.'

'Good.' He picks up his sports bag and tears off to the gym.

I wait eagerly for the next day. Unusually, Alex is already in his place, his head bowed. And that's how he remains. He says nothing to anyone, never raises his head, doesn't once look up.

The week after. It's raining and I want to get across the school yard quickly. Alex is standing there. He holds out an envelope. 'But only open it at home. Promise!'

'Promise.'

Now I'm home. The paper is still damp from the rain, the writing a bit smudged. But I can read it.

'I'm a shitty arsehole. I'm a gay. I didn't want to be. At first I puked. But now I've got used to it. But I'm also scared. Perhaps God hates me. Because of my grandma in Italy, I used to like God quite a lot. Now I just don't know. Is God cross with me? And what will happen then? I'm scared, because I don't want to die. Can you pray to God for me about all this? Alex.'

Six days later. Alex comes to meet me on the stairs.

'Have you read it?'

'Yes?'

'And?'

'What do you mean by "And?"?'

'Have you prayed about it, I mean.'

'Yes.'

'And what does God say? Is he still cross with me?'

'God doesn't speak to me as clearly as that. But I believe that he's not very cross with you.'

'Do you really believe that? But can you pray for a bit longer?'

'Yes, for God to be with you when you're afraid.'

'Is that all.'

'Yes, that's all.'

Two weeks later the holidays come. I say good-bye to the pupils one by one. Alex stretches out his hand to me, beaming: 'I think it helped. You know what I mean. The day after tomorrow I'm going to my grandma. In Italy.'

Tart! – So what?

Julia rushes down the stairs screaming hysterically. Hot on her heels are five girls from her class, yelling, cursing, 'Whore! Tart! Damned tart!'

They throw her school bag after her, pull her hair, tug at her sleeves. Julia hurls herself into my arms: 'Help me!'

'What's going on here?' I thunder at the five raging wildcats.

'That Julia's a whore, a goddamned whore!'

'Can you explain?'

'There's nothing to explain. On the class outing, ask the others . . . almost all the boys. She fucks around . . . And now also with Pedro from class 9!'

'So what?' I said that, and was almost as surprised at myself as the girls were.

'Don't you think it's bad that she has it off with everyone?' Even Sonia, who is usually so placid, is indignant.

'Why does a girl sleep with a boy?' I ask.

'Because she loves him.'

'Precisely. And if you love someone, that's wonderful.'

'And if you don't love him?'

'Then it's sad – because you long for love so much and don't get it from anyone.'

'That's true,' says Sabine softly and seriously. It's certainly an experience that she knows.

Suddenly we're all standing around somewhat helplessly. The atmosphere of moral indignation has gone.

'Here,' the active Draga gives Julia a handkerchief, 'blow your nose.'

'Sit down.'

What in the world am I to teach after this prelude? Talk more on the subject? I'm afraid of a new outburst.

The fat red Bibles are in the bookcase. I get them out.

'What, read the Bible now?' They feel just as much as I do that that's out of place.

'But we've never done that before!'

'I know, that's why we're doing it now.'

I have to search until I find it, that story which is so like our story, in John 8. The lawyers drag her in, the women who was a sinner: she's slept with a strange man, and she has to be stoned for that. Why doesn't this Jesus condemn her? And what does he say? 'Let him who is without sin cast the first stone.'

'Does that mean that he doesn't care what you do? Adultery and so on?'

'No, it means that we never put anyone off seeking love with stones and curses.'

'And why does everyone then go away?'

'What do you think?'

'Perhaps they no longer dare to try anything, because they secretly know that they've all done shit.'

Sabine is thinking hard.

'Doing shit, I mean sin and all that – does it then have something to do with love?'

'Often yes. It has to do with the love that we seek because we don't have enough.'

By now we're all a bit exhausted. I let them go home a bit early. As they go out, I hear Sabine ask, 'Julia, today we're going swimming. Do you want to come with us?'

This sentence isn't thought out and contrived! It was truly spoken just like that, by a girl who half an hour previously would have liked to strangle another in furious hatred.

The fat Bibles are still lying on the table. I want to stroke them.

I put them back in the bookcase. Slowly, one after another. Gratefully.

In the midst of the mud – the flower

She goes downstairs with me, accompanies me into the street.

'Alexa, don't you have to go to gym now?'

'Yes, but I'm not going. I said I wasn't well. That's a lie – but what am I to do?'

'And why don't you want to go to gym today?'

'Do you want to see?' She lifts up her T-shirt. Bloody weals on her back. Takes off her neck scarf – I'd been wondering about that; it was such a hot day. Long scratchmarks and dark patches on her neck.

'Who?' I ask, horrified.

'My mother,' she says in a matter-of-fact way. 'She often does that. That's why sometimes I don't come to school. And I don't want the others to see it.'

'But surely that can't happen?'

'It does. It's been happening for a long time.'

'And why does she hit you?'

'I don't really know. Because of everything. But I don't get hit after six o'clock.'

'After six o'clock. Why after six o'clock?'

'Because after six o'clock my father comes home from work. Then she no longer dares to. Because then he hits her.'

'Does he also hit you?'

'No. He never hits me. Quite the opposite.'

'Quite the opposite? What do you mean by that?'

She looks away. Looks into the distance.

'Alexa, does your father sleep with you?'

'But not often. You must never tell anyone. Otherwise he'll go to prison.'

'Do you love your father?'

She nods.

'And your mother?'

'She beats me.'

'And don't you want to leave home?'

'Yes, sometimes.'

'If you really want to, you can. You know that here are homes where . . .'

'My doctor's already told me that. She saw that I was being beaten. But that's not on.'

'Why not?'

'Because my mother comes from Greece. And if my grandma and grandpa and the whole family there learn about it – it's just not on. At home there people are very fond of children. And if they hear that I'm going away because I keep getting hit, they'll all hate my mother. Then they'll think really bad of her.'

'And you don't want them to think bad of her?'

'No. Then she won't have anyone. No one loves her. And I don't want that.'

'Do you feel responsible for your mother?'

'What does responsible mean?'

'You don't want bad things for her, although she hits you?'

'She's sorry about me, because – she often weeps. And when she doesn't hit me, I sometimes love her. That's why.'

The next day Alexa is again absent from school. I plan to speak to her class teacher, but I can't find him.

She telephones in the afternoon.

'Have you said anything to anyone?'

'No, but I think it would be . . .'

'Please, no. Please, please no! That would be the end. Then I would run away. Or kill myself. Don't tell anyone! Promise?'

'Oh, Alexa . . .'

'Promise! You must promise!'

'And will you promise that you will tell me if you can, if anything happens?'

'Yes I will. And can I telephone you? Whenever I want?'

'Whenever you want.'

In the coming weeks I'm sometimes afraid to pick up the receiver. Is it Alexa? I'm anxious about my perplexity. The initial horror at 'such family conditions' has subsided, but my uncertainty has grown. Whereas after the first conversation it was still quite clear to me what should really be done here, now I'm less and less sure. The amazing readiness for suffering and love in the midst of the tangle of hatred and pain . . .

Thursday. Today we get out of school early. She accompanies me to the car. Stands there undecided.

'Shall we go for a little walk?'

I go out with her into the park. After yesterday's rain the

ground is soft. We walk side by side, don't say much. At the top of the hill I pause. There's a wide view, a wind, light shining behind the clouds.

'Isn't it beautiful?'

Seeking assent, I turn to Alexa. She's looking at the ground.

'Yes, just look at that daisy – in the midst of the mud.'

In amazement I look at the trampled grass, mucky with sheep droppings and cigarette ends. And, in the midst of it all, this little flower, intact, unpolluted, upright and white in the mud.

'I like daisies,' says Alexa.

'So do I. Very much.'

We look at each other. Notice each other – grateful for each other.

She's been away for a long time. Absent from school for two or three weeks. When she returns to school she looks pitiful and thin. In the afternoon she telephones.

'Were you sick for such a long time?'

'Not really.'

'But you were absent.'

'Yes. Now it's all changed. My father's left. Now he's got a girl friend.'

'Isn't that a good thing?'

'Good? My mother still cries. And she drinks. What else is she to do?'

'What about you?'

'Me? It's good that I'm not in a home. I comfort her.'

'Does that do any good?'

'No. I've telephoned my grandma in Greece. Perhaps we'll go back to our family.'

'Do you want to go back?'

'I don't know. But then my mother will have a family again.'

'Are there daisies in Greece?'

'I can't remember. Why?'

'Because you like them. And so do I.'

Last day of school. Alexa says goodbye.

'I won't be coming back after the holidays. We're staying in Greece.'

'For ever?'

She shrugs her shoulders.

'Perhaps. But I can write to you. Whether there are daisies – and things.' She laughs,

'Yes, write. Whether there are daisies – and things.'

We stop laughing. Feel sad about parting. Separating after a long year together, helplessness, filth and mud. But also this bright little flower. Alexa will write.

Sleeping together – that's filthy

Another unusual lesson. It began with my weariness. Why not simply let the pupils read for once, from their beautiful illus-trated school Bibles?

Abraham and Sarah had no children . . .

'We don't want to read. Please, what else!'

'What do you really want?'

'We want to ask you all kinds of dirty questions!'

'And what do you want to know, Brian?'

'Why do grown-ups fuck? Do they like it, or what?'

'When a man and a woman sleep together – is that dirty?', I ask back.

Almost all the children nod.

When next day the class teacher asks me to build in a sex education lesson, because it's really needed, I can only agree. I respond by asking for a double lesson.

I've brought with me a ring cake, candles, cocoa. In the pleasant side room we lay a birthday table for the eleven of us and eat the cake.

'Why do people celebrate birthdays?'

'To remember. And to enjoy.'

'Enjoy what?' asks Mirella in amazement.

'Enjoy life. Who enjoys everything?'

'Parents.'

'My grandpa.'

'God, perhaps?'

'I most enjoy myself.'

That's clear in the case of the very small but radiant Michael.

'And for us to be able to be born . . .'

'. . . parents must fuck.' Brian has produced the sentence. His bright and alert face has had a tormented look on it for some time. Mirella has sneaked a second piece of cake and is now standing in the doorway.

We try to think whether we know other words for 'fuck'.

'Screw' is the next suggestion.

'Have it off.'

'Make love.'

'Sleep together.'

'The words don't matter. What I really want to know is why they do it,' Brian insists.

Mirella opens the door and goes out.

'Where are you going?'

'Out. I don't want to listen to all this filth.'

She can't be persuaded to come back. She can stay with the class teacher nearby.

When we're clearing up at the end of our birthday lesson everyone has hot ears and happy eyes. We've looked at the anatomical doll and said a lot and asked a lot.

'Damned good thing that there's a birthday,' says Brian, now content, chewing on the last crumbs of cake. I think so too. But Mirella?

For days her behaviour bothers me. Her big brother has come back from Croatia, a colleague tells me.

'And what does that mean?'

'Of course one isn't quite sure. But he sleeps in the same room. The father was in prison for that reason.'

'For what reason?'

'You know.'

Yes, I know. Abuse.

'Do you think that's possible?'

'Possible? Probable.'

Renate howls. Mirella has stuck a pencil in her neck and made it bleed. I bring Mirella to the front of the class. As she goes past, she pulls René's chair away. His glasses fall under it and a lens drops out. I help him.

'Dirty pig. Just look, Mirella's smudged my picture.'

That's enough for today. I send her into the side room. Through the open door I see that she's lying down on the floor in the golden corner of sunshine. Things seem all right with her.

And with us. A peaceful lesson.

'Mirella, come back over here for the closing blessing.'

She obediently gets up, and stands behind Michael.

'God bless us and protect us . . .'

At the first sound of the bell, she trips Michael up, throws herself on the weak little chap, and starts fighting with him, panting. While I'm pulling her up she kicks Michael in the stomach, making him double up.

After school I speak to the class teacher. Mirella has evidently been hanging around, sees me and rushes up to me. I seize her by both arms and hold her fast.

'Why are you still here?', she asks in a familiar way – usually her language is rather formal and stilted.

'Because we've just been talking about you, you monster,' I answer truthfully, 'about the bad things that you keep doing.'

'But I'm not bad.'

'Not bad? Then what are you then?'

'I'm nice.'

'All right, you're nice.'

I'm on the point of making a joke about Mirella's niceness when I see that she's quite serious.

'Yes, it's true. I'm nice.'

Her eyes fill with tears. Her body goes soft in my arms.

'Mirella, Mirella, Pedro's waiting for you, he wants – you know what.'

That's Brian, who's forgotten his gym kit.

'Filthy swine!'

In a fraction of a second her body has gone hard as iron again. She chases Brian with a raised fist.

I watch her go; now I'm fighting with tears. For a moment we both knew, Mirella is a nice girl. Whatever evil is done to her, whatever evil she does, in the depths of her being Mirella is nice. God bless and protect the little monster.

Sometimes I think that mum likes me after all

Afternoon. The telephone.

'Doro, is it you? How are things?'

'Terrible. Quite terrible. I've wasted my whole life.'

Somewhat astonished at this choice of words I ask back, 'How do you waste your life then?'

'My friend's gone off. For ever. I said, "Piss off, you arsehole" – and then he shook me and went away for ever.'

'Does that surprise you?'

'What else was I to say to him?'

'You wanted to swear at him, but you didn't want him to go away?'

'Yes. No. It's like this. My mother saw me with my friend. She only thinks that I sleep with him, and then she beats me. She doesn't know that I never want to sleep with a boy again.'

'Never again?'

'Since that time. On my tenth birthday. Then I was raped.'

'Does your mother know about it?'

'I think so. But perhaps she's forgotten. She never mentions it now.'

'And you haven't forgotten?'

'No, never. It was my birthday and I was to take something to my uncle. He works in a disco. And a big boy was there. He looked very nice. He went out with me and then suddenly he put his hand over my mouth and tore my dress and then he did it.'

'Did you tell your mother?'

'At first I lied. I was so afraid. I said that I'd fallen off the wall. And then I didn't stop trembling and the blue mark and every-thing . . . and then I told her. We went to the doctor. He said I can't get pregnant because I'm still too small. And then my mother was relieved. First she wanted to go to the police, but my father – my father – he was so mean . . .'

'Your father?'

'Yes, he said, not to the police. Probably it was my own fault. He was so mean.' She begins to cry. 'My mother shouted at him and he hit her – all because of me. But they wanted to separate anyway and now he's been away for a long time, that damned...'

I interrupt her. 'Doro, I find these swear words such a strain, and perhaps your friend does too.'

'Why? My mother uses them all the time. Besides, it's quite different with my friend.'

'It's different with him?'

'Yes. The only problem is that when I go walking with him in the wood – when he puts his arm round me I always begin to tremble, and then I tell him to leave me alone – because it makes me think of my tenth birthday. But he doesn't understand.'

'And if you try to tell him?'

'Now it's too late anyway. He's put an end to it. Yesterday, now that he's got a car – and I said he wasn't to drive so fast, and then he speeded up. And then I said, Slow down, or I'll open the door. Then he stopped and came round and I shrieked at him to piss off. And then he drove away and left me standing in the street.'

She goes quiet. After a while, I ask, 'And now?'

'I telephone you because I'm thinking, because I want to go away.'

'Go away?'

'Yes, I don't know where.'

'And that's why you want to talk to me? I think it would be better if we spoke properly, and not just on the telephone. Can you come round the day after tomorrow?'

She gets a bit of paper and writes down my address.

The next day she's absent from school. The day after that I hear that she's in hospital. Her mother has thrown her down the stairs. That afternoon I visit her in hospital. I visit her often in the three weeks that she has to stay in, and watch how she blossoms. She enjoys being looked after, enjoys playing with the younger children in the ward, enjoys the conversations.

Today I've brought her a box of Mackintosh's toffees. There's already one on her bedside table.

'From my mum. She's already visited me a couple of times. She's still fond of me. Sometimes . . . sometimes I think she likes me after all.'

A stay in hospital at the right time.

I'm sad – because now I'm no longer a virgin

She telephones in tears. I can already recognize her from the sobs.

'Has your mother beaten you again, Maria?'

'No. Yes. But it doesn't matter.'

'Doesn't matter?'

'I fell against the table and my ear started bleeding. Then I ran off and went to the doctor. I got beaten again for that.'

'Again?'

'Mum said that I wanted to tell on her. I don't. But the doctor has already asked twice, because I'm always so blue and scratched. That makes mum afraid – she's not interested whether I get hurt. But there's something far worse.'

'What's worse?'

'I'm pregnant.'

'Are you sure?'

'Probably, yes. Because I haven't had my period and my friend . . .'

'What about him?'

'The mean dog! I want to kill him. He's so mean.'

'Because you've slept together?'

'But we haven't!'

'Then you can't be pregnant.'

'But, because . . ., because . . ., the mean dog. He can do what he likes with me, he says, because I'm a foreigner, because my parents come from Spain. And I want to give him up because he keeps tormenting me. And then he said that I'm going to have a nice surprise. In eight months or so, and I should look at my belly now and then. And then he said that at the party I was blind drunk because he had put something in my drink, and then he slept with me.'

'Is that true?'

'How should I know. After all, I was drunk. His friend who was there grinned in a mean way and also said other things. I was knocked out. I just don't know. My mother wil kill me. I'm so terribly afraid. Sometimes I pray, but that doesn't help for long. You have to pray so often. What shall I do if . . .'

'First have a pregnancy test.'

'And if . . .'

'We'll think about the "if" after that. And telephone me when you get the result.'

Over the next few days I keep catching myself thinking about the 'if'. What if she is expecting a child? Is abortion a solution? No solution? What solution? We'll think about it then – I try to put it out of my mind.

Maria runs across the school yard to me, radiant. Whispers to me, 'I'm not – you can guess.'

During the lesson she keeps looking round, as if a load was off her mind. Afterwards she puts a note in my hand: 'Are you at home? I want to call you.'

She telephones.

'Good, you're there.'

'Now, does the world look better?'

'Yes. Do you know, my mother asked whether I was out of my mind. Because when I came home from the chemist's I was so happy, and she came to the door and I hugged her. She was utterly amazed – because I never do that. Still . . .'

'Is there something else?'

'Yes. I'm sad – because now I'm no longer a virgin and I never noticed. Is that bad?'

'Bad? So you're sorry about it – I can understand that.'

'And my girl friend, Nurgöl, is scared to death. Her father's a Turk.'

'And does that make her scared to death?'

'Yes, because she went with me to the chemist and – she's pregnant.'

'What will she do?'

'We don't know. I told her to pray. But she's Turkish. Is it all the same to God?'

'Yes. You're Spanish and Catholic; she's Turkish and Muslim. For God it's all the same. Praying is good – but she should do something else as well.'

'Can Nurgöl come to see you although she doesn't do RE?'

'Yes, bring her along, and we'll think . . .'

'I know another girl who is also . . .'

'Maria, just Nurgöl – just the two of you. No one else.'

Why no one else? I ask myself on reflection. My strength isn't enough for everyone. There are advisory bureaus.

But there's something else. The children come because they want to be taken notice of and because – unexpected though it may sound – they hope that God sees their distress and will help them. And I am to be the channel and the guarantor for that. But I can't be. Time and again they find me indicating: you're important to me; I know that you're good in the depth of your being; whatever you may do, I take your anxiety, your rage, your grief seriously – but I can't help you. I can't help you in the sense of putting an end to things, changing them. And when they often hope, full of hope and anxiety, If I pray, will God help me then? I communicate to them, It's good to pray, but God doesn't help.

What a brutal message!

With me they have to learn and endure the fact that this God does not simply do away with bad conditions, pain and anxiety, but remains with us in them.

'. . . even if I walk in the darkest valley, you are with me.'

The valley will not suddenly become bright, but we need not be alone in the darkness.

Then they sold him

I feel at the end of my strength and my imagination. 'Unless I learn to hear the coarsest swear word with the same tranquillity as I hear the word "daisy" I shall never be a useful teacher.' Exhausted on a Tuesday afternoon I write this down in my school preparation book.

When I enter the classroom I hear a bitter dispute:

'Tart.'

'Wanker.'

'Whore.'

'Pussy-licker.'

'Dirty pig, lick yourself.'

I firmly shut the door and announce: 'Shut up, we're going to begin.'

Fabio shrieks with indignation:

'But Sylvie is a dirty pig. I'm not a pussy-licker. Tell her that she's a pig.'

'She isn't a pig, but stupid. Anyway, no one licks cats.'

Amazed silence. Eleven pairs of eyes look completely perplexed. Then eight-year-old Manfred takes the initiative. Don't you know what a pussy-licker is? Shall I tell you? It's a cunt-licker.'

'Thank you,' I say, 'and now let's stand up to pray.'

By powers of good protected wonderfully,
confident, we wait for come what may.
Night and morning, God is with us, faithfully
and surely at each new born day.

Fabio pipes up, 'Is that true? That God is always with us?'

'Yes, Fabio,' I say, 'always.'

Wednesday. Today seems to be an orderly lesson, I think, until suddenly one of the little baskets with grains of corn – the corn that Joseph distributes in Egypt during the seven years of famine – flies through the class. Hundreds of grains of corn fall everywhere.

'That's enough,' I say, rush to Fabio and seize his fist. He is now in process of crushing one of Joseph's brothers, who is made out of green plasticine. I would have liked to smack him, but instead I take him by the shoulder and turn him roughly towards me.

'What on earth has got into you?'

Stubbornly, almost full of hatred, he looks at me. For some seconds we are enemies. 'God is with us night and morning,' I think. In my head I hear Fabio's question, 'Is that true?'

'Yes,' I had answered. 'O God,' I think, 'then be here too. I'm about to hit him. Or I must get out.'

I didn't need to get out and we had a peaceful end to the lesson, with many fat and thin clay cows, which Joseph's brothers seemed to be guarding.

In the evening I look through the exercise books. Fabio's book, which began quite cheerfully at the beginning of the year, has become increasingly thin and confused since Christmas: the writing has gone to pieces and the pictures are black and chaotic. What's up with him?

And what's up with me that I came so near to hitting him? Meeting his violence with my violence? I'm sorry for him. Sorry for myself.

The next day Fabio is absent, and for the rest of the week. I go to the class teacher. Is Fabio sick?

'No, Fabio's in a home.'

'In a home? So suddenly? Why? Surely he has parents?'

'Maybe, but he's in a home. Don't bother about the details . . .'

Children come into the classroom and we break off.

I meet the head in the garage.

'Can you tell me what's up with Fabio?'

'He's been taken into care.'

'Does he steal?'

'If only he did! No, he was on the streets. His father sent him out as a rent-boy.'

'Is it true that God is always with us?' Fabio asked, and I said 'Yes'. I said 'Yes' and almost hit him because he was vulgar and violent. Vulgar and violent. Fabio – sent out on the streets by his unemployed father.

His book was still on my desk. The last sentence in it ran: 'Joseph was sold. That was a very bad thing for him . . .'

Here's our archangel – piss off!

Advent. I've brought some pictures of the Annunciation, a big one to hang up and around it twelve smaller ones, all different. Different, but also the same: the angel, usually coming from the left, attention focussed completely on Mary, who in many pictures seems to turn away, shocked, at least suspicious. We look at the pictures.

'Why isn't Mary delighted by the angel's news?'

'What's an angel? Do they exist?'

'Why is there a lily on every picture? Why not a rose or a sunflower?'

We look for answers. Angels. What are angels? Beings of light, messengers of God, helpers of people. What does that mean in our life? And the lily – a sign of purity, of innocence?

'The angel Gabriel in particular is often depicted with a lily,' I say.

'What? Is he called Gabriel? Gabriel – and innocence!' Daniel is vastly amused.

'What's so comic about it?' I ask.

'Gabriel! Don't you know Gabriela? She lies and steals and plays truant. She and an angel of innocence!'

'Where is she, then, this Gabriela?'

'In the home.'

When after the first term Gabriela came back to the class, I was keenly interested in her.

There she sat. Her wild locks covered almost all her face, a stubborn mouth, sad eyes. No one wants to sit next to her; they prefer to squash three to a desk, together. A trip to the planetarium has been planned for the next lesson.

'Piss off,' snorts Gabriela to Daniel, who chances to be walking next to her.

'Stupid tart,' he retorts crudely.

'Fuck your mother.'

'Fuck yourself!'

Before I can intervene Gabriela pushes him and he twists her arm, so that she lands on the pavement. In the planetarium she sits a row behind the others.

Since Gabriela has come into the class the general tone has got much cruder, in a way which leaves me at my wits' end.

Today the boys have a long sports lesson. I'm alone with seven girls. We push the seats together and sit in a circle. There's a place free next to Gabriela. It looks a friendly circle, but I don't feel that it is. 'For the last few weeks it's been cunt, fuck, shit, kicking and hitting,' I say, 'I don't want to go on like this.'

'It's only because Gabriela always . . .'

'Shut your mouth, you arsehole . . .'

'Listen to the blessed angel Gabriela, ha ha!'

'No one does so much lying and stealing and . . .'

A chair falls over, Gabriela rushes to the door. I go after her. I grab her in the corridor. She resists. We both land on the floor. Weeping loudly, sobbing, she keeps talking: crying, accusing. I send the others back. She lets me hold her. Takes my handkerchief.

'Come on. We'll cope. Let's have a proper conversation some time.'

She gets up, comes back with me.

'Look, here comes our archangel again!'

Martina didn't mean it maliciously, but it's enough for Gabriela to hurl herself on the girl, shrieking, to pull her hair and rush out of the class. Howling loudly, she runs down the stairs to the exit.

Something in me explodes.

'Are you all completely crazy?' I shout at them, and scold and upbraid them as never before. I sit down. They're silent. So am I. For minutes.

'What shall we do now?' asks Monica softly.

'Nothing.'

'We can't just do nothing.'

'Yes, you can.'

I go to the window. They're waiting. Still silent. After a while I say, 'You can do what you want. I'm not teaching today.'

The very next day it's RE again. The boys are back. The girls are still very subdued.

'Gabriela is absent.'

'You were really furious yesterday.'

'Yes, and today we must talk about it again.'

We do so. Finally, Alexandra from Greece says, 'Perhaps Gabriela will be less spiteful if we do something with her. And next week I could sit next to her in RE.'

Something like a sigh of relief goes through the class.

And the miracle happens. Since Alexandra has been sitting next to her, the venom around Gabriela has disappeared. Even the class teacher notices that there's something approaching peace. For two or three weeks.

Vigorous knocking at the door. A stocky man bursts in with a very red face and thick wavy hair.

'Excuse me, I have to know just one thing. Who are the girls who were eating ice-cream with my daughter yesterday?' He looks around, seething with resentment.

Gabriela is cowering, like a terrified little wildcat.

'We're in the middle of a lesson. Perhaps you could come back afterwards . . .'

'I must sort it out now,' he interrupts me curtly. 'Who was eating ice cream yesterday with Gabriela?'

Alexandra puts her hand up and, after some hesitation, so does Monica.

'So, you were at the ice cream parlour. And who paid?'

'Gabriela invited us.'

'Invited you, did she? She's stolen the money from her mother. Invited by a thief. Just wait until you get home!'

Snorting with fury, he leaves the classroom.

'Gabriela's often given us sweets or bought us an ice recently. I thought it was her pocket-money,' explains Moni.

The class is over, and so is school. Gabriela is still hanging around. She's afraid to go home.

'Should I come with you?'

'No, better not.'

'Have you often been stealing money?'

She nods.

'But not much. I don't get any pocket-money because my parents say I don't need it.'

Perplexed, I pack my bag. When I come out of the teacher's room she's still standing there.

'I have an idea. Every Tuesday I'll give you ten marks. And you'll stop stealing. Shall we try it?'

She shrugs her shoulders.

'Do you want to think about it?'

'I'll give it a try.'

We shake hands. The hint of a smile crosses her face.

My face, however, may have looked relatively dark as I drove home. Since when does one provide a good education with money? But what is 'a good education' in the face of brute violence from parents? Still, couldn't I have had another idea? Isn't it a blessing that Alexandra and a couple of others no longer exclude her? And isn't it understandable that Gabriela wants to give them something in return, sweets, an ice? Doesn't it look as if there's been a breakthrough from this vicious circle of rejection and hatred?

The success proves me right. The class is less complicated than it's been for a long time; the level of cursing and aggression has dropped; there are no more complaints about stolen money or pencils. Until – one afternoon my telephone rings: Gabriela's father. He's found money in his daughter's purse, 'and now the crafty thing says that you've given it to her.'

'That's right.'

'How dare you! My daughter has all she needs. She gets food, has respectable clothes. She doesn't need anything. She doesn't need money of her own.'

I concede that the business of ten marks was an unusual measure and that I should have discussed it with him.

'I would never have agreed.'

In the background I hear dull banging and loud weeping.

'Is someone there crying?'

'Yes, you can hear it. I locked Gabriela in the bathroom. After I'd punished her . . .'

'You hit Gabriela?'

'Certainly. I've a right to. After all, I'm responsible. I was beaten as a child and it never hurt me. And I got plenty of it.'

'Gabriela is a girl and already thirteen.'

'Do you think I want to bring up a slut? It doesn't matter how old she is; if she doesn't obey, that's what will happen. Moreover I've forbidden her to go with the group to the children's farm.'

'But I'm going with them!'

'Indeed, that's why she's looking forward to it. And that's an end to this enjoyment. In the future she must be back home fifteen minutes after the end of school. I've plenty of time to check that.'

'You're unemployed?'

'Just for the moment. My wife works.'

'Can I speak with Gabriela for a moment?'

Amazingly he agrees. Opens the bathroom door. Sobbing loudly, she picks up the receiver: 'I'm not allowed . . . I'm not allowed . . . he's . . .'

'Is your father in the room?'

In answer she weeps loudly into the telephone, tries not to say any more. I've never felt more helpless. I can't touch her, can't ask her anything. I just say, 'Listen. I'm here. We'll meet tomorrow morning. Can you hear? . . .' At some point she hangs up.

She's pale the next day.

'Did it go on being bad yesterday?' I ask.

She shakes her head. 'He didn't do anything else to me.'

'Does he hit you, or does he also do other things?'

'Why do you ask that?'

'Because I've been wondering.'

'They always wanted to know that in the home. It's nobody's business. It's our family. And no one has the right . . .'

I'm completely flabbergasted by the defensive tone. Does she have to defend her father? She comes after me in the corridor. 'But don't tell anyone. I've said nothing to you. Do you understand?'

'You've said nothing. Not a word.'

'I haven't said a word. You can swear to it. Otherwise my father would kill me . . .'

She's summoned to a lesson, goes back.

Once again I go into the RE room. The picture is still hanging on the wall: Gabriel with the lily, the heavenly messenger, the being of light.

Isn't every child such a messenger from heaven?

How many blows does a child need to make her violent, how

much abuse does it take to destroy her capacity for love, how much untruthfulness until she is mendacious?

I take down the angel from the wall. What is he doing there?

'You've taken down the picture!' Gabriela is the only person to notice the next week.

In the new school year she's no longer in the class. Where is Gabriela, then? In the home.

I couldn't change, improve anything in her life. I couldn't help. Not at all.

And yet there is an angel who bears her name. And she knows it.

If my brother makes me pregnant, she'll kill me

The telephone rings. I pick up the receiver.

Sobbing, through which I can barely hear my name. More sobbing.

'Who is it? Martina. Is it you? What's the matter? I can't understand you. What are you're saying? Yes, you were absent today. Are you sick? Your ears – what's the matter with your ears?'

She calms down a bit. Now I can understand her better.

'My ears hurt so much, my head, the side where I got hit the most – but I'm calling because I'm so afraid.'

'Who are you afraid of?'

'Of . . . I don't know. Of everything.'

'Has your dad hit you?'

'No, mum. She's my stepmother. For just a month. And yesterday she hit me with a boot. So hard and so long that I thought I was going to die.'

'What had happened, then?'

'Because my father had hit her son – with the ladle, and made his forehead bleed.'

'And she beat you for that?'

'Yes, because – it was my fault.'

'Your fault?'

'Yes, because her son is now to be my brother. But he keeps wanting to sleep with me.'

She bursts out into incessant weeping. She sobs, sniffs, blows her nose, sniffs again.

Suddenly: 'It's like this. My stepbrother has dropped out of school and now he's bored, and whenever I come home . . .'

She begins to weep again.

'When you come home – what happens then?'

'Yesterday he cooked a lunch for me, and while I was still eating, he began. And he couldn't care a shit that I don't want to because he says he's not my real brother and besides, he says, I'm old enough.'

'How old are you then, Martina?'

'I'm fifteen and he's already seventeen. And he's much stronger. And we fought. I kicked him in the balls. I didn't want to, but then he let me go. Then I went into my room and shut him out. But then, but then . . . then he came in through the bathroom and throttled me and then . . . and then . . . he took off all my clothes.'

Now she's weeping gently to herself. I'm at a loss. Besides, in ten minutes I have to leave the house to catch a train. What can I do with this desperate girl?

'O God, if only you would rend the heavens and come down!' Is that in Isaiah? Wherever it is, rend the heavens! Come on, God! How should I, how can I, teach religion to this misery? I feel guilty, guilty at my impotence. This impotent God – shouldn't we keep quiet about him? We may pray to God, mediate, keep silent, but speak? Are there words which are enough to reach out of his reality into this wretched earth? Speak? I don't know what. Listen, anyway. Listening as a form of preaching. Even if I am impotent, can't help you, I won't leave you alone.

'Are you still there?'

'Yes, Martina, I'm still here.'

She blows her nose.

'And then, when my father got in from work, I told him, and he got so furious that he picked up the ladle and set upon my stepbrother and beat him up. And how! Then my stepmother came in. She didn't ask what was going on. She took off her boots at the door and shrieked that he was to let go of her son and fell on me. Hit me with a boot on the head, and it began to bleed. And she wouldn't stop. I look absolutely awful. So I didn't come to school. Do we have RE tomorrow?'

'Yes, there's RE tomorrow.'

'Good, then I'll come.'

'Then we'll see each other in the morning.'

The next week Martina returns to her real mother.

'She beats me too, but not as hard. Whenever she's furious that my father has gone off, she drinks beer, and then I often catch it. But sometimes she's also nice. Still, if my brother makes me pregnant, she says, she'll throw me out for ever. Then I'll kill myself.'

'Come to me first.'

'Can I live with you then?'

'No, not live – but we can talk and make a plan.'

'What kind of plan?'

'We'll think about that then.'

Martina didn't get pregnant.

Reflections

Someone says, 'I don't understand how one can be for years with these maltreated and abused children without getting dulled or simply breaking down.' Nor do I, but I do have a memory.

The walk with Alexa. 'Isn't it beautiful?' I ask and look up at the sky and out at the view. 'Yes,' she says and drops her head, 'Just look, a daisy in the mud.' Flowers from the trampled earth.

Children who are beaten, humiliated and sexually abused are 'trampled'. They experience violence in the everyday life of punishments and often in the dark night of sexual attacks. That these usually come from their closest relatives makes them defenceless and the trust inevitably becomes fear, wounds them in their humanity. Left to their parents, they often seem less worth protecting than animals.

Being exposed is the opposite to security. This experience of being in the clutches of others leads to a basic feeling of vague fear and latent threat. And do we wonder at the constant readiness of some children for aggression?

Others are wrapped in a deep weariness with life as in a grey cloak.

Nothing interests them, they enjoy nothing. 'Don't touch me!' is the only message that I read on the wall of their silence.

The obligation to keep quiet about interference from their parents amounts to their complicity in continued humiliations. The conflict of loyalty between love and betrayal, fear of losing the family, their only familiar place, often makes them prisoners of hell.

When eleven-year-old Laura who used to take part in the lessons in a cheerful and lively way would only stare ahead apathetically, and also became increasingly grubby, one day I addressed her directly. 'It's my family, isn't it?' was the aggressive reaction. 'Yes, but it's my RE lesson and you're stinking worse and worse,' I retorted equally abruptly. Then she began to cry. No, she couldn't talk to me about it. Yes, perhaps with her friend Anna. The very next lesson Anna came up; Laura wanted to speak to me. The other girls might be there but not the boys. The seven of us sat round a big table. And what came out was this. Since the summer holidays Laura's father had been creeping in to her at night. She was afraid and felt sore. She didn't dare tell her mother. Once her younger sister woke up. She told their mother. Then the mother beat Laura, threw her round the room and shrieked 'whore'. Since then, she had to go to bed without supper and without washing and no longer got any clean clothes. 'I believe she wants me to stink and go hungry,' said Laura tonelessly. After the mother once again half killed Laura by beating her, Laura went into a home. We talk on the telephone sometimes. When I asked how things were she said, 'Oh, you know, really quite good.' 'Really?' It came out hesitantly. 'I'm always homesick. But you can't have everything.'

No, you can't have everything. The homesickness of these children for a place where they experience trust and security will always remain unsatisfied.

And RE? A colleague is furious. 'Do you simply want to pray it away? Do you believe that all that blessing helps? Suicide – a total attack on humanity – has that anything to do with God?'

No, it doesn't. But it does have something to do with his crucifixion.

Rudi Dutschke put it like this: 'A slap in a human face anywhere in the world is a slap in my own face.'

Anywhere in the world where children are humiliated and shamed, they are crucified in their humanity, and the divine is crucified in them. I can't change that. I can only look at the resurrection experiences in life. Keep putting the healing love alongside the sick love: I can see you in your hurt, in your humanity, and I like you.

And then time and again it is these children themselves who show me that sometimes a bright daisy grows from the trampled earth. That much and that little.

3

But I'm Scared

Slashing people – that's fun

Again he's standing in front of me, Igor, this colossus of a boy. Both hands in his pockets.

'RE is shit – I can't bear it.'

'I know. And I can't bear your hands in your pockets.'

I'm clear that here I'm following an old-fashioned ideal of courtesy, but after all, Igor is telling me what he can't bear.

That was an almost stereotyped ritual from the beginning of the school year. Igor is so fat that he doesn't fit into normal trousers and always wears a kind of baggy tracksuit. Although he isn't stupid, he's avoided by his fellow pupils. Is it only his bloated body or his enjoyment of little sadistic torments?

Hands in his pockets again! I'm stupid enough to try to take them out. To do this I have to spread my arms out wide, as he really is extraordinarily fat. I'm nonplussed. No furious protest. Instead of that an almost delighted smile on his face.

Since that day there's been a new ritual. Instead of expressing his views on RE there is an almost benevolent 'Good morning', standing in front of me, legs apart, both hands in his pockets.

'Good morning, Igor. Take your hands out,' I reply just as benevolently, and take them out myself.

That happens for several weeks, at the beginning of every lesson. He evidently likes to be touched, not only in fighting and pushing, but also with kindly gestures.

Last week he had to go to the school head.

'What was that about?' his classmates wanted to know.

'Oh, nothing special. A couple of old women sneaked on me.'

'What was there to sneak about?' I now asked.

'Nothing bad. A couple of grannies hopping about. I just wanted to see whether they could still run. With a hose! How scared they were! They hopped like monkeys. And they got soaked . . .'

'Do you think that's good?'

'Why not? It's fun.'

'You're a horror. A real horror.'

Gerda hasn't been long at this school and finds its coarse customs difficult.

'Did you enjoy it when the little boy screamed because you cut up his teddy bear?'

'Yes, that's why I did it.'

'What did you do, Igor?'

'Oh, there was a boy in the playground with a teddy bear. A very old-fashioned kind. A scruffy old thing. I took it away from him and slit it open.'

'Slit it open?'

'With my knife. All the stuffing came out and the boy roared as if I was slitting him up.'

'And that gives you pleasure?'

Igor has drawn in his head between his massive shoulders. Now his eyes are small and evil, but a smile of enjoyment plays round his mouth.

The next morning he's again standing in front of me, hands in pockets. That makes me contrary.

'You can leave you hands in your pockets. It doesn't matter to me. If you're constantly using them to torment people . . .'

'I don't do it all the time, I . . .'

'It doesn't matter. Sit down.'

He drops heavily on to his chair. He always sits at a desk by himself, because there isn't much room beside him. He doesn't join in this lesson. He broods away darkly.

Before the summer holidays an expedition is planned. Grilling sausages.

'We can surely spare ourselves the sausages.'

'Only because you don't like meat,' protests Sven.

'You don't like meat?' I'm surprised, for Igor's body doesn't give any hint of asceticism.

'No, it makes me feel ill.'

'Has it always done?' I'm really interesting in where this vegetarian trait comes from.

'No, when I was little, in Poland, I still ate meat. Until my rabbit . . ., until my father . . .'

Igor breaks off. Looks around, almost fearfully.

'What happened to your rabbit?'

'Damned shit!' He almost screams it out.

'It was *my* rabbit! My uncle gave it to me! He even had a name. And then my father . . . The mean dog. He massacred him. The fur over his ears and that was that.'

He's silent. Sunk in on himself. Now he sits there like a small boy. Very small and very helpless.

'And you saw it?'

He nods.

'And then I had to eat some. He beat me because I didn't want to. And then I was sick. And then he really beat me and locked me up. In the shed. Nothing to eat for a day. The mean dog.'

'And since then you haven't eaten meat?'

'What?'

He's miles away.

'Oh, the sausages for the outing. It doesn't matter to me.'

At home I thumb through the books from 7a. Igor began his in January. It's remarkably complete. He was making a real effort and then wrote whole pages in his distinctive curly writing. I read the first page.

'When I think of the future – I prefer not to. I can't imagine it. If it's beginning now I think that it's puke. Like the past.'

I want to talk to a colleague about Igor. There's nothing special about a child having a rabbit, which is killed; that happens thousands of times, he says calmly.

My colleague is probably right. A child's love, a child's mourning is despised a thousandfold; there is a host of children who protect themselves with an armour of unscrupulous aggression against a future which they already find puke.

A future of puke. Igor had written that in January. Now it's July.

I meet him at the bus stop that afternoon.

'Have you any plans for the holidays?'

'No. Nothing doing. And my youth group's going away too. Three weeks camping by the North Sea.'

'Why aren't you going with them?'

He shrugs his shoulders.

'Dough. Were would my parents get that from?'

I telephone the pastor. Could the parish perhaps pay half the costs? We discuss it.

Last day of school. I say good-bye to each pupil one by one, because I don't know whether I will be having them next year. Igor's big, soft, rather moist hand . . .

'By the way, I'm going to youth camp after all. Some feeble-minded person has forked out the dough for me.'

The words may sound dismissive, but the boy is radiant.

After the holidays I meet the youth leader.

'How did it go with Igor?'

'He surprised us completely. He was particularly good with the little ones. No, he isn't an angel – but we can use him. And another thing, he was in the water even in the coldest weather. After all, he's got a good layer of insulation on him.'

Precisely: a fat body, which is both a protection and prison for his wounded soul.

Chaos and the blessing

They listen intently. How will this battle with the Amalekites in the wilderness turn out? Will they win, or will Moses' people?

Then José has another of his crazy turns.

A pencil has fallen down; he reaches for it between the chairs, pinches Claudia in the leg, and tips out a school bag, hurling the books into the air. In this state he can't hear. So I fish him out, hold him very firmly.

'Go on with the story!' ask the others.

I hold José and go on telling how Moses climbs the mountain – in the heat and the dust – raises his arms to God and . . .

'José's pulling faces all the time!'

For a couple of minutes he's enjoyed being held, and has leant on me; now he wants to get free again, wriggles and fidgets in his attempts to do so.

I put him at the back of the room with wax crayons and a painting pad, and go on with the story: 'When Moses couldn't hold his arms up any longer, he saw . . .'

'José's throwing the crayons around.'

That's enough. I send him out. He won't go. I take him out, but he claws at me, won't be shaken off, kicks the door, rattles the door handle, knocks over the wastepaper basket. I'm at the end of my strength and my patience.

'For crying out loud, José, what do you really want?'

'To play,' he says simply with a serious look.

José is one of four children in a family and lives with his parents in two and a half rooms in a busy street. They have no garden, no balcony and no space to play, but they have a TV and a video. At the beginning of the week José's attacks are particularly severe.

Play then. I quickly put seven or eight books on the floor in the corner, draw white chalk lines between them and give him an empty drawing-pin box. 'Here's your car, and those are your friends' houses. You can drive along the white roads to visit them.'

'But now do go on with the story!'

The other children have observed José's special treatment with quite amazing patience. This time it seems to have worked. Brmming gently, hopping up and down, José drives his drawing-pin-box car through the chalk streets. Then he gets louder. He begins to sing, louder and louder:

'Shitty pants, cunt chaser,
fuck and screw
with your dick.'

'Stop singing that! You're disturbing us,'

'Can you hear what he's singing?,' asks Eric.

'He's been singing it all the week.'

'Shut up now, José.'

He looks up, amazed. Deadly serious I think. Then his features are distorted in a foolish grin; he waggles his head, pushes the books away, spins around on his bottom and kicks anything within reach. Now this also gets to the others. They kick back. In an instance I'm beside Jose, trying to stop him hitting out vigorously about him.

'That's enough. If you can't behave like a schoolchild . . .' I shake him, don't know what to do.

The bell rings. The others get up. 'You can go.'

'No blessing?'

'No, not now. I can't.'

'But you said that you people can always pray, even when driving cars,' Anette recalls.

'Nevertheless, I can't now. This evening I shall say the blessing for you.'

'For me too?'

'Yes.'

'And for me?'

'For you too.'

'And for me?'

'Yes. I shall think of each one of you.'

They go. I sit with José in the devastation on the floor. Chaos.

'I want to go to break with them.'

He kicks and struggles to get free.

'I know, but first we must clear up here.'

'OK.'

I let him go. He picks up two books and like a flash he's out of the door.

'Can't catch me!' he shrieks back.

No, I can't. That was enough. Thanks to his friends Moses could ward off defeat by the wild Amalekites. My defeat by the wild José is complete.

Exhausted and sad, I clear away the books and crayons, and today I must also put up the chairs all by myself.

End of school. I go to the garage. José comes running behind me.

'Wait!'

I wait.

'Will you do something for me too?'

'What should I do?'

'You know – this evening?'

'The blessing? Am I to say the blessing for you too?'

He nods vigorously, turns round, and runs yelling after the others.

Some weeks later he tells us that his family is going home, to Spain. He doesn't like it, he's quiet and oppressed.

We practise Psalm 23. José, despite his fit, was the first to know it by heart.

'Do you want to say it?'

José does: 'The Lord is my shepherd,

I shall lack nothing.

He feeds me in green pastures,

and leads me to fresh water.

He refreshes my soul

and puts me on the right way. . .'

'When you're in your country and we say this psalm, then we can all think of you.'

'Will you really?'

'Yes, we really will.'

That was eighteen months ago. Class 3 has become Class 5 and Psalm 23 has become the José psalm. One of the children keeps suggesting that we say the 'José psalm'. New pupils are amazed. Then we tell them about José, how bad he was, all the things he did – and it usually sounds very loving.

Recently Petra had to go in to hospital. She's afraid.

'Will you say a psalm for me too?'

'Let's think which.'

By now, as well as Psalm 23, we can also say Psalms 139 and 91 by heart.

May God protect you with his wings,

may you find refuge under them,
may no harm come to you,
may no misfortune approach your dwelling.
For God has commanded his angels
to preserve you on all your ways.

Yes, we'll say Psalm 91 for Petra while she's in hospital.

I think of that lesson eighteen months ago which went completely wrong, of my defeat as a teacher and a person, sitting on the floor in chaos, incapable of anything and unable to say the closing blessing.

Without this defeat sixteen children would not have learned about the possibility and the power of intercession. José the untameable, José the bad boy, we owe it to him.

I prayed – but I'm still a failure

That Mike! He's already sixteen, gangling and lanky. His twin brother is at grammar school, two classes above him.

This difficult boy has two faces. Either he broods gloomily or he fools around in an irritating and malicious way and gets not only on my nerves but also on those of his classmates. Today we're talking about Martin Luther King, the bus strike in Montgomery. I have the pupils' full attention.

'Who's this Buddha? Why don't you ever tell us about him?' Mike suddenly bursts out.

'Buddha? How did you discover him? Are you interested in Buddhism?'

'I don't know, but that Christian God's rubbish. Doesn't do anything. My grandma always prayed with us. And what happened? I'm still a failure. Stupid school. May as well do myself in. I've no future.'

'Don't begin all over again,' says the cheerful Liesl. 'All this nonsense, suicide and that.'

'After all, you're not the only one at this school. We keep you company', Tony consoles him.

'And now do you want to know something about Buddhism?',
I interrupt.

'Buddhism, or whatever it's called – I don't care. But Buddha.
Who was he really?'

'All right, I suggest that today we finish talking about Martin
Luther King . . .'

'Don't finish anything. Talk about Buddha now!'

'Is it so important?'

'Damned important.'

I don't ask why and begin to tell simply what I know: of the
protected childhood of this young prince, rich and handsome,
shielded from all suffering, his secret excursions and his first
encounters: with old people, with the sick, the dying.

Mike listens, leaning forward with literally an open mouth.

'Why, why did he leave the palace? That was quite crazy.'

I attempt an answer: 'He wanted to understand suffering, this
bad suffering of men and women and their fear.'

'And? Did he solve the puzzle? – Shut your mouths.' He snarls
to those sitting next to him, who are whispering to one another.

Once again I'm teaching for only one pupil.

Happiness, riches, success, power – Mike nods: 'Yes, that's
what we want.'

'And the Buddha recognized that this greedy effort is also the
basis of our fear, that hunger for this life is the cause of pain and
suffering . . . something like that.'

'And did he also say anything about suicide?'

'I don't know.'

'But if I kill myself, that's an end to fear and so on.'

'But that's not what the Buddhists believe . . .'

'Now the idiot's back to his suicide,' moans Regula, on edge.

Anyway, the lesson is just ending. Mike wants to know one
more thing.

'Can you pray to Buddha? Is that a sin?'

'A sin? Certainly not.'

'Would you do that?'

'I don't do it. There are quite different ways and that's not
mine.'

The bell rings. Mike comes to the front.

'That kind of Buddha figure, I mean, a little one, can you buy them?'

I promise him that I'll find out.

At coffee with friends one evening I tell them about this unusual quest for knowledge and the difficult pupil's concern.

At the end of January a friend telephones. She was in India and remembered Mike and his wish: she's brought back a little gilded Buddha for him.

I hang on to it for a week. Mike had said that the God of the Christians is 'rubbish'. Should I further emphasize that by offering him 'another God' to worship? Won't he become even more disorientated? But didn't I also say that there are different ways? Mike is in spiritual distress, and he's seeking, if not a way, a path, a track out of the jungle of suffering, humiliation and fear of the future.

By now it's February. I take the tiny Buddha to school.

'Is that for me?' Mike exclaims, almost horrified, and blushes. 'What does it cost?'

'Nothing. My friend brought it back from India for you.'

'Truly, from India? As a gift?'

'Yes, from India and as a gift.'

It's the first hot days in May: Mike is wearing only a T-shirt. On a thin black leather strip round his neck I recognize the little Buddha.

Almost a year later. A group of youths in the tram. I recognize Mike by his voice. He's also seen me. He's now an apprentice. Yes, things are going really well. He unbuttons his anorak and brings out the leather thong: 'This little chap is really good. That was the only good lesson with you. It really gave me something.'

He gets off at the next step.

'Bye then.'

He turns round again, and gives me a cheerful grin over his shoulder.

The angel in the T-shirt

Most pupils help in the preparations for the summer festival. Only five slouch into the classroom somewhat disconsolately.

'I have an African set of Happy Families – do we want it?' I ask.

'Great!'

'Then we don't need any books.'

'Hey, we're playing something,' Peter shouts down into the school yard.

They all sit in a circle; only Pascal continues to stand by the window and stares out.

'Come on, we want to start.'

'Shit stuff. Don't fancy it.'

'Why "shit"?' I ask as calmly as possible.

'First, I don't know how it goes, and then Africa. Africa! The damned niggers should shove off and leave us in peace.'

Sullenly, he finally joins the circle and drops onto a chair so that it makes a noise. Changes chairs. The second isn't right either. The third is.

How difficult I find this boy! Spoilt, sullen, underhand. His far too fat, pink body is always in a fashionable outfit, T-shirts with lurex, trainers with lights at the back. And his eternal eating!

He puts two lumps of chewing gum into his mouth at once. Now things seem to be going better with him. We play, laugh, joke. Splendid, Marlies has the first family.

'You've been bloody awful, so mean. I'm not going to play any more. You can have your muck.'

The cards sail over the table

'I haven't been bloody awful,' Marlies defends herself, shoves Pascal.

'Damned cunt, if you touch me you'll get such a punch that your guts come out of your mouth.'

Seething with rage he stands there, his flabby body vibrating. I catch his upraised fist. 'That's enough. If you don't want to play, then sit there and copy out yesterday's text.' We go on playing, but the fun has gone out of it.

'Just look, now he's blubbering.'

He really is. He's lying over his book and sobbing, as if he's been done a great injustice. I send the others out for the break a bit early.

'Now, Pascal, tell me . . .'

'Just don't blabber any shit at me!'

He raises his head with a defiant jerk. In the process of energetically rebuking him, I am horrified by the look of profound sadness on his tearstained face.

'Tell me, what really is the matter?'

'What's the matter? What's the matter? I'm muck to you. Muck. Shit on your shoes. Muck for everyone. They're all mean. They all get at me, and now you're doing it too. I'll kill myself. I don't care. Then you'll see. You'll all see. So mean.'

His taunts are swallowed in sobs.

'Look, I want to say something to you . . .' I touch his shoulders.

'Hands off,' he shrieks hysterically. 'Anyone who touches me will get it.'

That was clear. I sit on the table next to him. The blinds are down. It's almost twilight and intolerably hot. Pascal weeps. Suddenly he gets up, knocking over the chair and going into the group room next door. The door is open but I can't see him. Nor can I hear anything.

This experience of helplessness. No advice, no course of action, nothing goes. Not even time. A standstill. Heat.

I wait. Am I waiting? Waiting for nothing. Is that also waiting?

'Are you still there?' Pascal is standing in the doorway. 'Why are you sitting around?'

'I don't know. Tell me, do you have a friend?'

'A friend, no. Anyway they're all arseholes. And idiots. My father says so too.'

'Idiots. Is that what your father says?'

'Sure. It's an idiot school, isn't it? And that's why my father is cross with me.'

'Why is he cross with you?'

'Because he can't stand idiots. And who will take over the firm if I'm so stupid? So he keeps hitting me.'

'Your father hits you?'

'Hit. You know what hit means? With electric flex. And then at night I have to sit on the chair.'

'At night? Why at night?'

'To learn discipline, my father says. And last night . . .'

His lower lip trembles.

'What happened last night?'

'When everyone was asleep and I couldn't sit any more, I wanted to creep to my bed. But it was only a trap. Then the mean dog came and hit me so much that I thought that I was going to die. He kicked me. The shithouse. How I hate him.'

Pascal has now stopped crying. He stares ahead. Hopelessly sad.

Hopelessly. I don't know a way either. Conversations, social security, aid? Is there something which could keep him from getting reconciled to failure? His whimpering heart which unloads itself in brutal blows, the desperate soul which expresses itself in obscene cursing. The humiliation which he wants to shake off by handing it on.

'Do you really want to stay here for ever?' His voice suddenly sounds very clear.

'No, let's go.'

'OK,' he says, 'Bye. Till next week.'

'Bye, Pascal.'

At home in the evening. That calendar has been hanging there for eighteen months; time to change it. Russian icons. I thumb through them.

Strange. Surely I've seen that angel recently? Rubliev, Moscow, fifteenth century. Now where have I seen that angel? The sorrowful eyes, the round cheeks, the soft lips, almost firmly closed. The red garment, the wings with blue lines. Wings? No, Pascal's broad white T-shirt has no wings.

But the face, it's his face!

Pascal, an angel? I hang the calendar up again.

Icons – a window on eternity it says on the cover. The 'Pascal icon' looks at me. I look at it. A window on eternity.

Pascal, you too are a window. You who are quite unique, meant by God, accepted.

And I can't accept you? I can find no way to you. My soul has got tangled up in your flashy clothing, your coarseness. I've been distracted by your crude language, your balled fists, on a journey which leads away from you: troublemaker, problem pupil. And now this angel.

I look at him for a long time. The faces overlap. Pascal's face, the face of the angel. Precisely!

School the next day. The pupils come leaping down the stairs to meet me during the lunch break, Pascal in their midst. The angel in the T-shirt! I have to laugh. I laugh at him.

Then he comes up to me, breaks his chocolate bar in half. 'Here's something for the break for you. It's got a bit white, but that doesn't matter.'

No, it really doesn't matter. Thanks, Pascal.

Wild, *that great remark by Martin Luther King*

Martin Luther King. The pupils think it's bad the way the blacks are treated in the bus; they can't understand that blacks weren't allowed to go to the white schools, scandalous that they couldn't get into restaurants or cinemas.

'That Martin Luther King was simply super,' Victoria remarks.

'A pity that they bumped him off; he might have thought of a solution for Yugoslavia as well,' reflects Drago.

'I like that wild sentence best,' adds Alex.

'What sentence do you mean?' I ask.

'I find it really wild that those who take the sword perish with the sword.'

'Can you say in your own words what's so good about that?'

'Yes, that it's no use if the crazies beat or gun down each other. Just look at Yugoslavia. The Chetniks do it to us and we do it to them. Afterwards they're all fucked. So I think Martin Luther King is a really good type.'

Well, I think, the language doesn't really matter so much; they've understood in their hearts what non-violence is all about. I feel good. It's good that there are such lessons.

The bell rings. The others come in. Scuffling in the doorway.

'Get away!'

'Do you mind!'

'Filthy dog!'

'Say that again!'

I can't stop the fist which lands heavily on Ali's face. Blood spurts from his nose. The two get all tangled up: hitting, kicking, hair-pulling.

'Alex, Ali, stop!'

They don't hear me. So I shove my body into the tangle; they notice this and stop. They stand there panting, smeared with blood. Big Alex is howling with rage. Ali's nose is dripping blood on the floor. He rubs it with his foot.

'Tell me, Alex, you said that you thought that remark about the sword such a good one . . .'

'What?' he says in perplexity. 'That's got nothing to do with it. I don't have a sword, and besides, Ali is a damned Turk.'

'Just don't begin that again!' Ali raises his bloodstained hand threateningly.

Quivering with hate, Alex hisses, 'Just wait, in the break I'll smash your face in; I can tell you, you'll be soaked in blood.'

I would like not to have to teach the next lessons. Not because of the spots of blood on my pullover; I feel as if I've come from a battle, one which I've lost.

I'm nobody

Peaked cap pointing down his neck, hands in pockets, shortly before the beginning of teaching a big fair boy comes in and plants himself by the door.

'Who are you?' I want to know.

'Me, I'm nobody.'

'You look to me quite like somebody, but I don't know you.'

'You won't get to know me. I don't go to RE. Your shit God,

as far as I'm concerned he can . . . So that's that!' He turns round
and bangs the door behind him.

'He's quite new. He hates RE; he gave it up in the other school.
Besides, he's furious.'

'Furious?'

'Yes, his old man's doing time. Grievous bodily harm or something. It was even in the paper. After that Manuel didn't come to
school for two days.'

'Is his name Manuel? God with us.'

'What's he got to do with God?'

'Him? I don't know? But his name, Emmanuel, means God
with us.'

'Damned if it fits him,' remarks Mike.

We have the lesson. Today more bad than good. Manuel's
sorry, stubborn departure has taken away all the interest, even
the friendly warmth which sometimes helps to replace the actual
interest. Nothing seems important. There's a grey desolation that
I can do nothing with.

I give out a text:

I believe in the sun,
even if it doesn't shine.
I believe in love,
even if I can't feel it.
I believe in God,
even if I don't see him.

Lines scratched on a wall in the Warsaw Ghetto.

The Warsaw Ghetto. That means nothing to the pupils. The
fate of the Jews, that means nothing either.

'He doesn't have a mother either,' says Otto to himself.

'Mother? Who doesn't?'

'Manuel of course.'

'Oh, Manuel. Now you can stick the sheets in your books and
we'll finish.'

'Can I have another sheet?'

'Mike, haven't you had one already?'

'Yes, but I thought – I could take one for Manuel.'

'He'll throw it straight into the waste paper basket.' Otto shakes his head.

'He might,' agrees Mike, 'but perhaps . . .'

I give him a sheet. 'You're right. Perhaps . . .'

Believing in the sun even if it doesn't shine, believing in love even if I don't feel it, believing in God even if I don't see him . . . impossible? Difficult, anyway. But perhaps . . . Emmanuel . . . God is with us.

What do I expect from the new year? Shit

The first lesson after the Christmas holidays. The new year is a whole week old. What will it bring us? What are we looking forward to? What are we afraid of?

'I'm afraid that my parents will get divorced.'

'I hope that my grandma doesn't die.'

'Perhaps my friend will come back from Italy.'

'I'm afraid because of the war in Bosnia.'

Some play a lively part. Others don't join in. So I distribute sheets of paper and let them write things down.

What I read that afternoon, clumsy and unadorned, is the anxious anticipation of a gloomy future.

'What do I expect? Shit. What else? My father's out of work.'

'What will the new year bring? What indeed, if my parents are already fighting at Christmas?'

'My friend has Aids. I'm scared.'

Boris has written a particularly large amount.

At this point I must break off and address the reader directly. What Boris wrote down is so gruesome and horrifying that right until the last moment I didn't want to include it in the book. I was disgusted and also ashamed.

But to distance oneself out of horror, looking away, leaves these children in a vacuum in which they seek to save themselves from the feeling of a void in life with ever coarser provocation. So let's try to read this description of Christmas afternoon by a delicate thirteen-year-old with a gentle face.

'My parents and my sister have gone away. Then my friend comes. He had a live mouse. We filled it with juice until it was dead. Then we dug up my sister's dead rabbit. We stuffed it full of Christmas bangers, spread out the fuse and blew it up. The half-rotten skin was hanging all over the bushes. It was really great. What do I expect from the new year? Nothing.'

I've no idea how I'm going to deal with this report in class. I'd prefer to pass over it. Not yet more details. On the way to the shops I see Boris. Although it's cold and raining he's going round on his bicycle without hat or gloves.

'Boris, where are you off to?'

'Nowhere, really.'

I think of the rabbit ripped to pieces. It's unbelievable that this boy with the soft face . . . I look at him. He seems frozen – and lonely.

'Do you want to come with me? I live nearby.'

He looks up in amazement.'

'I haven't any plans, anyway.'

We drink cocoa and eat cake; rather dry after Christmas, but it tastes good to both of us.

'Tell me, what you wrote, did you make it up or did you . . .?'

'We really did it. You probably don't have strong nerves if you find it so bad. You should have seen the video . . .'

'Do you watch many videos?'

'Quite a lot. My father is very strict. Before, he always used to thrash me. Now I get house arrest. Recently for a whole week.'

'And then you watch videos?'

'Sure, what else?'

Are words any use against these images, this abomination which are poured out over him?

It gets dark early. I light two candles. Boris cautiously takes a woodcut in his hand, a family tree of the Makonde.

'From Africa? You can see how they all belong together. But now I must go. Otherwise it'll be arrest again.'

He puts on his anorak, which is still damp.

'Couldn't we one day in school, I mean all together in the class, drink cocoa, have the candles and so on?'

'You mean breakfast together? We can discuss that tomorrow.'

Everyone is in favour. Next week, first lesson on Wednesday. Everyone wants to bring something.

Already on the way to school I can recognize them by their plastic bags.

'I've got ham!'

'And I've got Nutella.'

'My grandma baked a Greek honey cake, specially for us.'

The table is laden with delicacies. I've brought candles and give Boris the taper. Almost reverently he lights the candles.

All fourteen sit down. A moment of uncertainty.

'Now we must pray,' proposes Christina.

'Do you pray at home before eating?'

'Only on Sundays, or festivals, when the whole family is together as we are now.'

Christina from Italy has a very big family.

We fold our hands, and say the prayer that we've always said at the beginning of the lesson since the start of the school year.

God, put your hands on my shoulders,
speak into my ear,
pour your love into my heart,
and help me to fulfil
your plans for my life.

Afterwards things are lively and enjoyable. Even the clearing up that we have to go on to do is amazingly harmonious.

What does an hour of peaceful togetherness count for in the face of a future threatened with destruction? This question raises its destructive head when I get home in the afternoon after a long school day. An hour of warmth and peace. I can't undo the terrible reality by setting an idyll against it. But I can keep setting another reality alongside it, let them experience that peace and security are also utterly real and possible.

Is it worth the effort? What can such a single hour achieve?

As much as the light of a single candle in a dark room.

I don't fancy such a shitty life

I've lost my key ring. That's really bad. The fuss, the cost, if the locks of three schools and three underground garages have to be changed doesn't bear thinking of. All my searching and questioning remains fruitless. I'm depressed, and even more so when in the afternoon I read about young car thieves. Didn't Rodrigo ask only last week whether one could break into cars with teachers' keys? I thought it a joke.

Next morning – after a bad night I get there early because I have to find a parking place on the street – Petra comes up to me: 'I found your keys! Over there in the bushes.'

I'm speechless.

'Aren't you pleased?'

'Of course, Petra, but how did the keys get in the bushes?'

'You're not really pleased.'

'I am. I'm very relieved and very grateful. It's marvellous that you found them.'

She smiles at me, somewhat shy, somewhat confused.

Something doesn't seem quite right here.

After greeting the class I take the bull by the hands. 'My key-ring disappeared yesterday. Did any of you take it?'

Silence.

'Petra found it behind the bushes. How did the keys get into the bushes.'

'I didn't throw them into the bushes,' Rodrigo is defending himself, although no one has accused him.

'But did you take them?'

'Only for a joke. I wanted to see what happened. And after the break I put them back at the front of the table.'

'And how did the keys get from the teacher's table into the bushes?'

Much shrugging of shoulders. Only Petra is red and staring past me with a glazed look.

'Have you any idea, Petra?'

Then she puts her head on her arms and begins to cry. Cries like a little girl.

'She probably threw the keys there herself,' says the pert Jessie, who lives in a kind of permanent feud with the melancholy Petra.

'I can't imagine that. Petra, tell me, what's the matter? Why are you crying?'

Amid the sobs it all comes out. The keys weren't lying in the bushes but on the table in the classroom, and she thought that I would be pleased if the next day . . .

'When I've been worrying all night long then I'll be particularly pleased and be very very grateful to you. Is that what you thought?'

She sobs pitifully. She should. This way of gaining my attention is very exhausting for me.

But I also have a bone to pick with Rodrigo.

'What were you really thinking of?'

'Nothing. I'm evil anyway.'

'Nonsense. You're a good-for-nothing, utterly. But not evil.'

'But I am evil. Perhaps I'll become a criminal. Or a fixer,' he adds in an almost childish way.

'Who says that?'

'My mother – I don't mind if I die anyway. Because when I die I'll see God. My grandma says so.'

'So that's what your grandma says?'

'Yes, she knows all about God.'

'And are you interested in God'

'I love God, and I want to see him.'

'But you still want to be a criminal too?'

'Not necessarily. But if my mother says so, perhaps I'll become one.'

The key ring has been completely forgotten.

'Is it true that you see God when you die?' asks Gina. 'I don't mind being dead either. In any case I've had enough of life. What's it for?'

'Isn't there anything that you enjoy?' I ask her.

'I don't know what. I've never heard or seen anything that's worthwhile. Life's shit. Nevertheless, I'll won't commit suicide again!'

I look at Gina. 'Not again?'

'Yes, last year. I was even in hospital. But after that it was such puke that I won't do it again.'

'And why did you do it?'

'Oh, my mother kept threatening me; she told father in the evening if I got a bad mark, or was cheeky or something. Then dad would hit me in the evening. And because I was always so scared of that, scared all afternoon, I often took tablets, only one or two, and went to sleep. Then I didn't notice being scared so much.'

'And did your father hit you then?'

'Depending on his mood. Sometimes he only laughed when mum told him what I'd done, but if he was in a bad mood then he really raged at me.'

'And then you wanted to kill yourself?'

'Wanted to? I suppose so. It was half a mistake. I simply took more tablets than usual and still more – and that's when it happened.'

Petra has long stopped crying. Her chin on her hands, she listens attentively.

'I often want to die too. I keep going up to the fourth floor and standing by the window. Sometimes I think I'll do it. Then I think of my grandma in Würzburg. And I stop. My grandma loves me. She is the only person who really loves me.'

'I don't think anyone loves me,' reflects Leo. 'I could be dead for all anyone cares. I just want to try out a few things with love and sex. But otherwise, I don't fancy it.'

'Do you like living?' Gina asks directly.

'Yes, though I sometimes find it difficult.'

'Were you beaten by your father?'

'No.'

'Were your parents divorced?'

'No.'

'Out of work?'

'No.'

'And they aren't foreigners either. So you can't really say anything.'

She's probably right.

The task for next week: 'Life . . .'. They are to complete this sentence and add two or three others. On one sheet I read: 'Life is fear and difficulties. Real shit. You can't understand it because it's somehow crazy. The world is finished anyway, and that's why I'm afraid.'

I bring a text with me for the next lesson: 'Human existence is built on fear, distress and death. The world in which man lives cannot be rationalized; it is incomprehensible and absurd. The mood shows man his inner insecurity and thus leads him to fear. In this fear his whole being is put in question.'

A few words have to be explained, then Leo says, 'The man is absolutely right.'

That 'the man' is Kierkegaard means nothing to them. But I am very interested that Kierkegaard from this desperate state sees the leap into the absurd paradox of faith as a possibility.

How can I go on teaching RE in view of the insecurity and meaninglessness that is experienced in daily life?

So in this lesson too, we say our old prayer:

God, put your hands on my shoulders . . .
Pour your love into my heart,
and help me to fulfil
your plans for my life.

What, God, do you intend for the life of these children?

Rambo in search of God

I get a new class. Really only a group of Class 3. There are to be nine children. But what rushes in through the door, pushing, fighting, grunting, is more like a herd of young rhinoceroses. After quarter of an hour everyone is at last really sitting on his or her chair – so they are children after all. I want to get to know their names. Sabine and Christian, Drago, Sonia, Alex – and you?

The little boy shrugs his shoulders: 'Don't have a name.'

'Well, what shall I call you then?'

'Doesn't matter.'

I make some suggestions: 'Felix? Or Frog King perhaps?'

The other children are enjoying the guessing game. The pale little thing twitches his eyes nervously and waves his arms around.

'Now, what do you want to be called?'

'Rambo!'

The weedy little boy has a very loud voice.

'Tell me, in the afternoon do you watch much TV?' I ask him.

'No, TV is boring. Usually video. I have my own – I also watch in bed. On TV I watch the Catcher films. Do you watch the Catcher films too?'

'No.'

'Why not?'

'Because I don't have enough time, and anyway I don't want to.'

Now he gets up, my 'Rambo' who is really called Andy, and says, shaking his head with concern: 'You're safe watching them. Even if they hit each other very hard – they don't really mean it. You needn't be afraid.'

His eyes have opened wide.

I ask, 'And who does really mean it?'

'The others, who really hit each other.'

'Your dad?'

Andy nods, 'Mum too. And uncle . . . but on the television they don't mean it. You're all right watching that.'

Is it perhaps even a blessing that Andy – at the age of nine – has his own TV with video so that he can escape into a world where people only hit each other for fun, whereas nearby they're fighting in earnest?

Next lesson. End of school. Andy-Rambo trots along beside me.

'I want to ask you something.'

'Yes?'

'Is there a God?'

'Yes.'

'Do you know him?'

'A bit.'

'Do you sometimes talk to him?'

'Yes.'

'Can you see him?'

'No.'

'Where is he then?'

'That's a difficult question. God is also in you.'

'And in you? And in everyone?'

'Yes.'

'Good. When I grow up then I'll cut peoples' heads off and see if I can see God in them.'

'Andy . . .'

'I must go home now. Bye.'

He runs down the street. He stops at the traffic lights. I see him shrugging his shoulders. As if he wanted to shake something off.

Sarah the skunk

All children paint. Deep wells, in which a little Joseph holds his hands up high.

'He's sitting down there in the mud – that would make me sick.'

The mud is zealously enriched with worms, frogs and beetles. They're almost enjoying the disgust of little Joseph.

'I can smell how the well stinks,' says Costa quite contentedly.

'My well stinks too.'

Something really is stinking here. I open the window. It's penetrating,

Vigorous sobbing. Sarah lies over her book and weeps in a heart-rending way.

'What is it, Sarah?'

'I've done it again in my pants. And if I shit myself I get it with the strap.'

She stands up and hurls herself impetuously into my arms. Her pain is greater than her stink, so I forget it for a while.

'Hold me very tight,' she sobs, and presses her snotty face into my stomach.

I hold her tight with my left hand and write on the board for the other children.

The well is deep. Joseph is scared. No one helps him out.

Writing is still a wearisome business for Class 2 and they take quite a while.

I take Sarah to the washbasin. No, she doesn't want to go to the toilet. There really isn't all that much in her pants. She wants to sit on my lap. But I don't want that: I have another two lessons after this.

'But take me in your arms,' she asks.

That's all right. I lean against the wall to support the pressure of her firm little body and put my arms around us. She still stinks quite a lot.

'Are things bad with mum when you go home with dirty pants?' I want to know.

'Mum isn't at home.' Heavy sobbing. Broken sentences.

'She only comes to shower, then she makes herself up and goes out again. – Because she's afraid if her boyfriend comes back – because he hit her in the stomach and tore her dress – because he wants money. And she shrieked and I had to get the police.' Sarah lets go, stands up, and says proudly: 'I know the number of the police all by myself, 110.'

'How come that you know it by heart?'

Sarah finds dealing with letters and numbers even more difficult than the other children.

'My mum trained me. Every day. Because you always need the police.'

'And did you call them?'

'No – I just couldn't!' Loud howling. The other children look round.

'First Umberto tore the flex from the wall, then he opened the door, pulled me by the hair and threw me downstairs.'

I've forgotten the stink, sit on a chair and cradle the sobbing, quivering little bundle. The other children are utterly silent. For a long time. I can feel her blouse wet with tears.

'And then . . . and then . . . our neighbour called the police. And they took Umberto away. And mum puked and howled.

And now she's always going out – because she's scared. But I'm scared too.'

'Then who looks after you and gives you breakfast and lunch?'

'Our neighbour. But she keeps giving me red-arse.'

'Red-arse?'

'Whenever my pants are wet I get hit – with the strap when they're full. And then I have to wash everything.'

'Wash it yourself?' says pale Nelly in amazement, who herself has wet pants now and then.

'Doesn't your mother hit you, then, when you wet yourself?'

'No,' says Nelly, 'because I don't have one. And I don't want a mother who beats me. Come into the home too; no one will ever beat you there for having wet pants.'

Sarah shakes her head.

'No, then my mum will be all alone. I want to stay with mum.'

The bell rings. The children stand up for the final blessing.

'Does it help you to stop doing things in your pants if you pray?'

'No, Sarah, praying doesn't help that at all.'

'And mum staying at home and no longer getting hit. Does it help that?'

'No Sarah, not that either.' I feel wretched.

'Still, I want to pray – but you must take me in your arms.'

'Me too – me too.'

Sarah and I stand in the middle, the other nine children crowded around us in a firm embrace. God bless us and protect us.

For a moment we've forgotten the stink.

'Amen. You skunk!' That was Gregor. Is it going to start all over again? But he graciously helps her to put on her big school-bag and together they trot off to the door.

Then I'll die too

Project days. Most pupils are out with their class teacher. Only four from Class 7 come to RE.

'You'll all fit into the car – would you like to go to Monte Scherbelino?' I suggest.

'Scherbelino, what a comic word!' remarks Tonio, the Italian.

'When Stuttgart lay in ruins and many houses were destroyed, fifty years ago after the war, they piled up all the rubbish there. It became a real hill.'

We park below.

'Do we have to go right up there?'

'It only takes ten minutes to the top.'

'Is there an ice-cream stall up there?'

'No, ruins.'

They listlessly trudge along the way. An empty Coke can which they kick in front of them cheers them up a bit.

Finally we're at the top. Overgrown lumps of stone, the colossal remains of rubble and a wide view over the city. Exhausted by the short climb, they sit on the stones.

'Man, look! A swastika!'

There really is a black swastika smeared with soot on a big cut stone, directly beside the wooden cross which towers to the sky.

'Does the swastika really have something to do with the other cross? They look very similar,' reflects Simon.

'Sure,' Thomas is seldom at a loss for a word. 'You only have to break all four arms of the cross and you have a swastika.'

'First destroy the cross, then the houses – that damned Hitler swine!' Simon scratches round the swastika with a stick.

'It's the same with us,' broods Dragomir. He lives with his grandma, his family is still in Bosnia.

'First they always talk about God, then they destroy all the houses, and the people. The whole shit. Why are there wars?'

I very much want to get involved in these profound reflections. Then Thomas jumps up.

'Oh, just stop talking. Do you think we can find old weapons here, or bones?'

Suddenly he is wide awake.

'Hitler was a criminal. OK. Still . . . He had the power! I would also like . . .'

'What would you like to do?'

'Hit everyone – so that they died. Blood through all the cracks. Anyway, we've too many foreigners here. One day . . .'

I interrupt his tirade.

'Are you quite crazy?' asks Tonio in a relaxed way.

'Crazy? How? War's fun. Then I'll die too. It doesn't matter. As far as I'm concerned the whole shitty world can go to pieces.'

He gets up, and goes through the ruins in search of what he calls 'war material'. The others follow him.

I sit there. In front of me the big cross which points into the clear sky and the little swastika which only fifteen minutes ago I would have said points into a dark past. Really back? How past is this past?

Anyway, they hardly seem interested in the wide view. Depressed, I call them for the journey back.

Instead of a weapon they've found the rim of a car wheel, which rolls clattering down the hill. A cyclist is coming along. With a skilful throw Thomas makes the rim land just in front of him. Enjoys the cyclist's fright.

'Thomas, bring that to me . . .'

Even before I have spoken he's picked it up. It whistles just past Tonio's head, who is walking alongside Simon. With a speed I didn't think I could muster, I run after the rim, pick it up, and hurl it down the slope into the bushes.

'Why are you so uptight?' asks Thomas coolly. 'We're only playing.'

'You call that playing! You could kill someone.'

Then I see that Simon has blown out the light burning on the memorial stone by the path. I want to give up. What on earth has got into these boys? We've talked for weeks about Anne Frank, about Martin Luther King. So much Nazism, racism and inhuman violence seemed incomprehensible to them. It looked as if they had understand something. And now, outside the classroom, so much delight in destroying, terrifying, hurting.

They hear my muteness – and that's amazing.

'We can light it again,' says Simon in a conciliatory tone.

'We don't have any matches.'

'Thomas smokes, he's got a lighter.'

He reluctantly takes it out of his pocket.

'You smoke?'

'Smoke? Smoke pot!', replies Tonio in his stead.

'Just wait. You'll be sorry,' hisses Thomas maliciously.

The car is in the sun. Burning hot. They squash in. None of us says a word. Hot, aggressive, cross, sorrowful, that's how we get back.

The head is still in the teacher's room. 'Great that you used the opportunity . . .'

'Unfortunately it wasn't. What on earth is up with Thomas?'

'Thomas? His father disappeared a few months ago. Just vanished. No one knows where.'

That evening on the TV, a boy wandering through the ruins of his city, fear and hopelessness in his eyes. His eyes – they're Thomas's eyes. The same look. Hopelessness and unbearable fear – children whose world has fallen in ruins.

I'm crying because they once loved each other

'Why has Eva recently been so late for classes?' I ask the class teacher.

'Don't you know? Her father hit her mother again, so badly that she had to go into hospital. And now there's no one at home who cares.'

It's two weeks before Easter. I talk about Judas – the one who was a friend, a disciple of Jesus, who loved him and betrayed him.

'Why did he do that if he loved him?' the children ask.

I have to think.

'Judas loved him and formed a picture of him, had a certain idea of him. He had great hopes. This Jesus was to be a warrior king who would free the Jews from the Romans. But Jesus wanted to be a king of peace. That wasn't enough for Judas. Judas couldn't understand why he didn't drive away the enemy, didn't abolish poverty.'

'Nor do I. Why didn't he do it?' Mario wants to know.

'Yes, why not?' I wonder.

'He really didn't abolish anything, not wickedness and evil, not even sickness and dearth.'

'Perhaps because he's simply a man?' Mario goes on thinking.

'Idiot! Jesus isn't a man. He's God!' protests Andreas.

'He's a man with God inside – it's quite special, because we can't grasp God,' comments Johanna wisely.

'And did Judas betray him because he was too much a man? Didn't he want him to be more like God? Was that why he was cross with him?'

Mario is clearly interested in the treachery of a friend.

'Yes,' I say, 'that could be. If you love someone a lot and are disappointed, then love can turn into bitter hatred.'

'I know that,' says Eva softly.

'You know that?'

'Yes, my parents . . .'

She breaks off.

'Is there also hatred there?'

'Yes, and now they're getting divorced. Because – my mother is in hospital again. Do you think that once there was love there? Perhaps when I was still small?'

'Yes I do. It's because they were in love that they became your parents.'

'Now let's hear more about Judas!' interrupts Mario.

I go on with the story. Then we write it in the books. I see that Eva is crying.

I ask her gently.

'Are you crying because your parents fight so badly?'

She shakes her head.

'No, I've got used to that by now.'

'But you're still crying.'

'Because, because – I'm crying because they once loved each other – at least when I was small.'

Better dead than scared

Two of them bring great lumps of clay into the class. Today we're going to shape them into the Joseph story.

There are twelve brothers. I suggest that each child shapes a brother – yes, they can also be green and red. But Manfred decides to shape a well, and before I know it, instead of twelve brothers I have at least ten wells. In my thoughts I'm already interpreting them symbolically: wells – depths – water.

And really, André has already filled his clay well with water. Christina also runs to the water tap. I remind the children that there was no water in the well into which the wicked brothers threw Joseph.

Then Manfred says:

'But he was scared all night. Water comes into my well, then at least he drowns quickly. Better dead than scared.'

Struck by his remark I repeat it: 'Better dead than scared?'

Then André says to me:

'You've probably never been scared, because you're grown-up.'

The bell rings for break. As they go they're making plans for the afternoon.

'My father has a new video, with monsters and all that.'

Michele begs, 'May I come too?'

'That's all right by me; anyway, my parents aren't at home.'

Better dead than scared . . . is that the alternative for video children, now eight – and when they're eighteen, drug children?

I believe in love, even if I don't see it

The week before the holidays! Today it's particularly hot.

'Do we really have to do RE in this heat?' Milena is sitting lethargically on the window sill and has no desire to go to her place. I sympathize with her reluctance.

'Make a suggestion. What interests you in the heat?'

'We could talk about love, for example,' she suggests.

'We could,' I agree, 'but I'm afraid that love also has something to do with God, and then we're back at religion. Would that be a bad thing?'

'No, that wouldn't be too bad. But I mean love – or sex – and God doesn't have anything to do with that, does he?'

Marcus, who hasn't taken part in this preliminary conversation, intervenes:

'Can't we get on with the prayer – I want to sit down.'
Together we say our new prayer:

God, put your hands on my shoulders,
speak into my ear with your voice,
pour your love into my heart,
and help me to fulfil
your plans for my life.

Milena: 'Love also happens, but it hasn't happened to me yet.
But anyway, that's not the love we want to talk about.'

It turns into a particularly lively lesson – despite the heat. How
can I tell whether someone really loves me or just wants to sleep
with me? How do you deal with your parents when you're in
love? Is Aids a punishment from God? And contraceptives? I'm
amazed at how tremendously well informed they are, and open
to one another, while at the same time completely helpless.

What is important for this lesson is not finding answers but
getting through to the questions – which these pupils by no
means find easy.

The next day I bring a short text, 'Diary of an Expectant
Mother'. It ends with the sentence. 'I can't say that I'm really
looking forward to the child. But I'm also afraid of an abortion.'

'Abortion, I'd never have that,' exclaims Milena spontane-
ously.

'Abortion, never, that's sin,' says Marion.

'Surely it's stupid first to make a child and then kill it,' thinks
Bernd.

I'm amazed. I didn't expect this responsible, life-affirming
attitude in children whose remarks are otherwise so pessimistic,
often cynical. How is one to understand them?

Angela enlightens me.

'Do you know, if my mother had had an abortion, I wouldn't
be here.'

'Nor my older brother,' says Felix, 'my mother was only sixteen then.'

'That sort of thing runs in our family,' continues Milena. 'My sister is seventeen and pregnant, my aunt also has an illegitimate child and my mother was one too. If they'd kept having abortions . . . Why do they have abortions anyway?' she asks, suddenly becoming pensive.

'Because life is shit!'

That was Mario, who so far hasn't take part. He too is the only child of a young mother. He's often violent in an almost sadistic way. Although he has a lively understanding he seldom joins in, but usually sits there darkly brooding.

What makes me particularly fond of him I can't say. Despite his uncouth behaviour, his obscene language and even despite his cruelty towards weaker ones, he exudes something of the purity of a clear, dark blue. That may sound somewhat incomprehensible. But that's how it is. A pure basic foundation can be detected even in his most furious behaviour, which is never completely obscured by the turbulence on the outer surfaces of his being.

'Your life is shit?' I ask in reply.

'Shit and puke. Now we're also going away from Stuttgart. That's also a kid of abortion. One more damned time.'

The bell has just gone. This was the last lesson before the holidays, and I won't be having this class again in the new school year. As a parting gift I have a card for each of them, printed on it an inscription from the Warsaw Ghetto:

I BELIEVE IN THE SUN
EVEN IF IT
DOES NOT SHINE
I BELIEVE IN LOVE
EVEN IF I DO NOT FEEL IT
I BELIEVE IN GOD
EVEN IF I DO NOT SEE HIM

JEWISH INSCRIPTION
IN THE WARSAW GHETTO

Mario holds his card in front of him with great interest.

'I think that's really good.'

'You think the card's good? Which sentence is the most important for you?' I want to know.

'Which sentence? I couldn't care less about any of them. It's the barbed wire round the edge that I like.'

I leave the school with drooping shoulders. Two years RE with this class. Two years struggling with these difficult young people – all in vain? Does the reality of the barbed wire cut off, scratch away any experience of love?

Second day of the holidays. I have to catch a train. The door bell rings. I ask through the entryphone who it is.

'It's Mario. I just wanted to say good-bye.'

I run downstairs quickly. He's standing there almost embarrassed, the big lanky boy.

'Good to see you again.'

'Yes, me too. I mean, now we're going to Munich. So goodbye again. And – by the way – I don't find that card at all bad – the writing too.'

We shake hands, look at each other and grin – both confused.

Then he goes and I run quickly upstairs two at a time – not just because I have a train to catch.

'I believe in love, even if I do not feel it' – and even more if I do!

Be glad that you're not hit with the frying pan

Next week it's the carnival holiday. Two busy festivals have given us a rather early beginning to the holidays.

'So mean,' squeals little Maria, 'What's got into them? Time off in the middle of the week and then even longer holidays.'

Maria is a dear, somewhat puny child, but by no means a zealous pupil. So I'm quite amazed.

'Don't you like holidays then?'

'No, certainly not. Whenever my mother doesn't like something, she goes after me with the frying pan.'

'With the frying pan? Whatever for?'

'No reason for it, simply when she's drunk. And that's all the time. When dad is there at the weekend he protects me. But otherwise I get hit almost every day. Would you like holidays like that?'

Dolores gives her own commentary: 'Be glad that your mother uses the frying pan. My father hits me with electric cable, that's far worse!'

Holidays. While we enjoy ourselves skiing, walking in the mountains or by the sea, these children are afraid of the frying pan and electric flex. Others have it 'better'; when asked what they did in the holidays they reply: drifting around the shops, spent the whole day watching videos.

Holidays, one word with completely different contents. How far do we really speak the same language, teachers and pupils? It often seems to me that we live on different planets. How can understanding, communication, education succeed at all?

Marco: 'School is better than holidays.'

I'm amazed.

Marco: 'That's why I like going to school so much – because then I don't have to be at home.'

My mother – a whore

Diana lounges all over the table: 'I don't like RE.'

'What do you like, then, Diana?' I ask. 'Is there something that you like doing?'

'No – I simply don't like anything – shit school, the whole world is shit!'

Now she's sat down and her pretty face is white with rage and abhorrence at this world.

All of a sudden she has tears in her eyes.

'Diana, what is it? Is there trouble at home?'

Then it all bursts out.

'My father keeps calling my mother a whore. That's so nasty of him, really mean.'

'And don't you like it when he says "whore" to your mother?'

'But she is a whore, a damned whore. I hate her. I hate everyone.'

She puts her head down on the desk and cries loudly. The other members of the class are utterly quiet. A quietness like a cloak, wrapping them and warming them. I sense that they understand Diana's pain and anger from within; not in the way that I can.

In the next two lessons I read the story of 'Hans my Hedgehog' with them. How a rejected child finds happiness after all. They're right on the ball and keep giving me glimpses of a life in them which is often repudiated.

Day by day the distance between our middle-class school life and these children seems greater.

Are you also interested in God in your spare time?

It was Mario's birthday yesterday. I look out a specially beautiful stone and put it in the bag from which a child can pick a semiprecious stone on his or her birthday. It isn't quite fair, I think, when I put in the little amethyst; I'm favouring him – and recently he's been so particularly horrible, loud and boisterous. But I remember how in the last school year Mario would always stand by, panting with enthusiasm, when someone else was taking out a stone, how he let the stones trickle through his hands, held them against the light, asked whether they were valuable. Not very valuable, I replied. 'It doesn't matter, they're still very beautiful.' He was one of the very few children who had been interested in the names of the stones. Rose quartz, amethyst, tiger eye – he would repeat them. Now he's turned into a troublemaker in the class. Nevertheless, I so wanted to see something like interest, perhaps even joy, on his face again.

Sometimes I forget the ritual with the birthday stone, and the children have to remind me of it. Not this time.

'Mario, yesterday was your birthday.'

'So?'

I shake out the stones on the bench.

'Come and choose one for yourself.'

He messes around by the map stand, quite uninterested; doesn't even turn round.

'Mario, man – just look – I would take that one!'

'Its great! If I were you . . .'

Everyone except Mario stands round the table and gives advice. 'Don't need any – what use are they?' he mutters, and pushes past the table to his place.

'It was great weather yesterday. Did you have a bit of a celebration?' I ask.

'No. Why should I?'

'Did you get any presents?' asks Laura.

'No, why should I?'

'Weren't you given anything at all?' I ask somewhat tactlessly.

'No. Well, money.'

'How much?' curious Petra wants to know.

'Three hundred marks.'

'Three hundred, man! Fabulous!' snorts Sven.

'Do you know what you're going to buy with it?'

'No. It doesn't matter.'

'What doesn't matter, Mario?' I ask.

'Everything. The whole of this shitty life.'

In the afternoon I take my bag of stones away. No one has a birthday tomorrow. I can save myself the extra weight in my bag. The extra weight on my heart is not so easy to get rid of.

What is up with this boy? His blank eyes are dull, tricks which used to be cheerful have become coarse, and worse, often brutal. I sense that there is something other than concern for him. I'm sad. I really liked him despite his unruliness. Do I still like him so much, this destructive young rascal?

By now the sun has set. I switch on the lamp on my desk. This jumble of books and papers. What help is it? How can I prepare for these children? What can I achieve? What can I prevent? RE. Is there a more useless subject? I become utterly disheartened. What's the use? Isn't all my effort in vain? What does it matter?

A day later. There's a ring at my doorbell. Mario is standing there. He's brought a 'mate'. Both of them are soaked to the skin by a sudden shower of rain. 'We just happened to be passing by and we thought . . .' They hang their jackets over the heating and come into the kitchen. When I ask whether they would prefer juice or cocoa, Mario says, 'Now I'm fifteen.' – 'That's right. Does that mean you'd like a coffee?'

Then we sit with our coffee mugs in the living room.

'Do you live near here then?' I ask Mario.

'Not really far.'

'What does "really" mean?' I want to know.

'Well, last summer my father ran off.' Then the house was too big, and now Mario is living further away, in two rooms, alone with his mother – but he doesn't see much of her. Now she's working as a barmaid.

'And what do you do the whole time when you're alone?'

'Videos. What else? When the weather is good I go on the street and see if anything's happening. Those shit foreigners. You know.'

'No, I don't know.'

'They ought to be kicked out, they're taking everything from us.'

I know that Mario's father is a foreigner, an Italian. To remind him of that now would only underline the fact that they take everything away from us: he, my father, has taken everything away from me – familiar surroundings, home, a mother who is at home in the evenings.

I see that the two of them are hardly touching their coffee. Fortunately they're not too old for chocolate. Then Mario's mate says he has to go home.

'OK,' says Mario, 'we'll go.'

In his voice is all the hopelessness of someone who does not 'have to go home', because no one is there expecting him, no one who is pleased or at least cross when he comes in.

I get their jackets, which are still wet. Mario has picked up a book lying on the table: *What Kind of God?*

'Tell me, are you also interested in God in your spare time?'

'Yes, I am.'

'Oh well,' he remarks. 'We must go now. And thanks for the coffee.'

'. . . *until finally the police caught us*'

The unit for the lesson is 'Self-Interest – Community Interest.'

Lying. When do you lie? We've all lied at some point. Stealing. Have we also stolen? What's the difference from pilfering?

There's a lively discussion and everyone has an amazing amount to contribute. Finally Mario (a more peaceful and friendly pupil):

'I've certainly pilfered more than most. It was more like stealing. When you pinch things worth two thousand eight hundred marks, that's stealing, isn't it?'

I think that he's boasting, or he wants to lead us on to slippery ice.

'Mario! Two thousand eight hundred? How do you know the sum so precisely?'

'Because that's what the court said. I was up before the court three times.'

And then he tells the whole incredible – but absolutely true – story.

Four teenagers have roped in three nine-year-old boys and got them to steal systematically from department stores.

'They went round with us and pointed out the things that we had to steal: watches, walkmen, bags and that sort of stuff. Then they stood by the door until we had finished stealing and they said that if we ran off or told on them they would slit our bellies open. Once Peter howled and said he wouldn't any more, so they took him to their place and stripped him naked. Then we were all so afraid that we did everything that they wanted – until at last, at last the police caught us. Was I glad!'

'Why were you glad?'

'Because I was always afraid. Of the brutal lads and in the store and at night and always.'

'When did all this happen?'

'About two years ago.'

'And when did you come to this school?'

'About two years ago.'

'Which came first, the stealing or changing schools?'

'I can't remember. Does it matter? The main thing is that I'm no longer scared.'

(Of the three teenagers three went to prison and one was deported to Turkey).

Reflections

'Does it help you to stop doing things in your pants if you pray?' asks seven-year-old Sarah. And I reply 'No.' 'But I still want to pray, and you must hold me tight.'

God's helplessness and God's power are revealed in this brief dialogue between a desperate child and a helpless adult. God will not stop the dirty pants and the fear of being beaten, but we can hold each other tight. We can take each other in our arms and look at each other; we can forget the fear and the stink for two minutes and experience God for two minutes in the mystery of nearness.

The stories which I have collected in this chapter are no less than edifying. Because I have not – or have hardly – beautified them, they are crude – including the language. Children who believe that anyway they will become criminals because they're no use, who call a father a 'mean dog', who couldn't care less if they themselves 'kick the bucket', since the world is 'rotten anyway' and the future brings 'nothing but shit', these children suffer life to a degree which passes our understanding. Those who become exposed to them, in other words who do not simply concentrate on the teaching material, are brought to the limits of their own capacity for suffering. For me there is only one redeeming feature: looking for the special child even in the most difficult child.

As well as the everyday impact of violence in war, on the television and in the family, some children experience that their parents are utterly disorientated. They hardly know any compulsory patterns of life or even rules of behaviour. On being asked 'When do you eat at home?', an eight-year-old says, 'What do you mean, "When?" We all take something out of the refrigerator when we're hungry.' 'When I showed my dad the water pistol I'd pinched he just laughed,' related a boy in the same class.

This haphazard upbringing, even if it is understood as a free upbringing, gives the children weak and disturbed characters and in part makes them immune to feelings of guilt and shame. They don't feel free but exposed, exposed in a desert without tracks, without landmarks and boundaries. That is the only explanation I can give for the way in which they accept the immutable ritual of prayer at the beginning and blessing at the end so readily: there is security within fixed rules. Hand in hand with the loss of orientation goes the complete withering away of a sense of self-worth. Those who are given their own television or computer game instead of loving care at the same time get the message: you aren't particularly interested in me; you don't think I'm worthwhile. And so they go to bed with their video – and that isn't meant metaphorically – watch another disgusting shocker to send them to sleep and spend their Sundays with computer games in which by skilful killing they prepare themselves for life in a perverted society: hollow and brutal. And on Monday they return to school. The young people often say quite openly how good it is that the weekend or even the holidays have come to an end. School is a beneficial place of care and fixed rules.

The older they get, the more difficult it becomes for them to shake off experiences outside school. I ask myself whether they have any feelings of love, even of penitence or shame, at all; what feelings do they have apart from helplessness, boredom and hatred?

'Give it up, it's total nihilism,' advises a friend. 'It isn't,' I reply. 'As long as these children suffer, I can still reach them.' 'Those who cannot suffer must hate,' says H.E.Richter. The right to fear and mourning: RE as a place in which suffering is allowed. A new definition? We should try it out. How much suffering there is in the stories of the Old and New Testaments! I don't find recipes against suffering anywhere. I find many stories of how Jesus looks upon suffering and doesn't evade it; how he touches the sufferers.

4

Meeting Death – and Left Alone

Dead? He's snuffed it

Lisa comes into school weeping. Her friend, the one who takes drugs, has died. Last week.

'Dead? He's snuffed it. Croaked,' jokes Philip brutally.

'I won't have you talking like that,' I interrupt him.

'Snuffed? Croaked? What's wrong with that? They're good words. I'll snuff it one day. Perhaps quite soon.'

'Why do you believe that?'

'Because I want a fight. A punch-up.'

'Who are you going to punch?'

'Don't care. It's all the same to me. If anyone tries it on with me I'll hit him on the kisser and do him over. He may do me in. It doesn't matter. Snuff it or not. The main thing is to fight. – Best to begin with the teachers,' he adds aggressively and looks at me with tightly screwed-up eyes.

Is this hatred? Despair? Helplessness?

I've seen the same look once before. I remember. On a farm in Africa. They had caught a young leopard who was slightly wounded. Now he was sitting in a cage: useless power, wounded beauty, wild helplessness. God help us if the leopard breaks out of his cage, I thought at the time.

Lisa has been looking out of the window the whole time, unseeing.

'Do you want to tell us about your friend?' I ask her.

She shakes her head.

'But, he has a twin brother. No one could tell them apart. He also likes me.'

'Do you like him?'

'I don't quite know. But my parents won't allow it – though he has nothing to do with drugs. He just looks exactly like my friend. As though he were alive.'

'What really happens to love when someone is dead? Not in a film, but in real life?' Bianca wants to know.

'You can't love anyone who isn't there any more.' That's clear to Freddy.

'But my friend is still there – somewhere, anyway,' Lisa contradicts him and begins to weep again.

'At least in the memory. Or what?' Freddy likes simple answers.

'I believe that the soul, the inner being of a person, never dies,' I say, more to Lisa than to Freddy.

At the end of the lesson – to vigorous protests I had insisted that Philip took off his walkman and turned off the music – Philip of all people asks: 'Are we having RE tomorrow or is it cancelled?'

'No, it isn't cancelled.'

'Good,' says Philip with satisfaction and goes out.

I watch him go, shaking my head.

In the break I speak with a colleague. Philip's mother died when he was two. He has grown up in a variety of homes. Nevertheless, he was such a nice boy when he was little, she says. Now he's becoming increasingly brutal; he has a real hatred of life.

'Is he still in a home?' I ask, and learn that for six months he has been living with his father, who is proud that at the age of fourteen his son is a real man, knows about sex and cigarettes and can defend himself.

How does someone who is trapped and wounded defend himself?

A few weeks later Philip disappeared. He was caught at the Dutch border and sent back. He came to school only now and then. Then he completely disappeared. That was a year ago.

At least he has life behind him

RE first lesson. Doris, an attractive blonde girl, is sitting in a corner. She doesn't want to get up and go to her place. She grumbles, bends double, says she has pains.

'Have you eaten something bad?'

'No, it's my period.'

'Is it always so bad for you?'

'How should I know? It's my first.'

'Then, Doris, today is a very special day.'

'I could do without it. I think it's shit.'

She sits down on the bench and weeps.

'Tell me, what's so bad about it?'

'If you want to know, I can't sleep with my friend any more. Otherwise I'll get a child.'

Doris is thirteen.

'You're already sleeping with your friend?'

'Sure. Otherwise he'll drop me. Besides, he's the only one who is nice to me. My parents are puke.'

Some weeks later. The first lesson again. Doris stands by the window and stares out. She's very pale. Her movements are strangely mechanical as she sits down. We pray, 'By powers of good . . .' Doris mutters something to herself.

'What did you say?'

'It's all lies. I don't believe it – protected. Protected from what? My friend – my friend – he's dead.'

'Dead? Your friend?', I ask.

Everyone is horrified. Then Jens shouts: 'Dead. OK. Snuffed it. A fight, was it? At least he's got this whole shitty life behind him.'

Doris looks at him. Tonelessly she says, 'But I haven't.'

'When's the funeral?' I ask.

'Tomorrow.'

'Are you going?'

'I'm not allowed to. My parents have forbidden it. Because of drugs and all that.'

'Should I telephone your parents and have a word with them?'

'You can't. We don't have a telephone any more.'

'And if I go home with you after school?'

'No, please don't! Don't.'

She's gone red, is ashamed and clearly doesn't want me to meet her parents.

The next day in the classroom. The class teacher is clearly annoyed. Things are getting worse with Doris. She was in school for the first three lessons and then cleared off – without any excuse. This playing truant mustn't become a habit.

'Don't you know that her boy friend has died? Perhaps she's gone to the funeral.'

'Her boy friend? Not a word. Why doesn't she say anything?'

'Is that the business with the icepick in the castle grounds?' asks a colleague who is thumbing through the newspaper. 'In those circles . . .'

Next day she's back at school. Very much keeping herself to herself. Still, I ask, 'Were you at the funeral yesterday?'

She nods.

'Do you know something. It was such a coincidence. The priest said our psalm.'

> Lord you search me out
> and know me . . .
> Whither shall I go from your spirit?
> And whither shall I flee from your presence?
> If I go up to heaven you are there,
> if I lie down with the dead,
> see, you are there also . . .

'Do you believe that God is with him?'

'Yes, I do.'

Doris goes thoughtfully to her place.

My father – the ghost

Berto is a special boy. He stands out even at a school for those with special needs, where there are many special children, above all because of his eyes, which are always wide open in his very pale face.

I've already asked myself why he's at this school, since contrary to many of his classmates he reads and writes quite well – when he reads or writes.

He often stops in the middle of a sentence and stares ahead, which means upwards, with eyes wide with terror. If one then speaks to him he reacts in an angry and obscene way, throws his pencil down, kicks his schoolbag or hits the person sitting next to him.

In the autumn Otto tells the class about the festival that he went to with his dad. Then Berto interrupts him and says, 'My dad's always doing . . .'

'Liar! You don't have one!'

'Yes I do!'

'No you don't!'

'Say that again!'

Of course Otto says it again and in a flash there's a fierce fight.

Once peace has been restored I try to take up the topic of the perhaps absent father once again.

'Every child has a dad. But sometimes he goes away, then . . .'

Berto interrupts me:

'My dad hasn't gone away, he's always there, but he's a ghost.'

He looks at me, defiant and triumphant at the same time.

'Can you explain what you mean?'

Berto stands up in his place.

'It's like this. My dad and I, we were together in the car and then my father drove into the tree and there was blood everywhere. Then the car caught fire and my dad did too. He was unrecognizable.'

Despite his hasty talk he's gone even paler.

'And you. Were you there?'

'Yes.'

'And weren't you hurt?'

'No.'

In the break I talk to the class teacher. Yes, there was an accident, but Berto hadn't been there; he has this fixed idea, which he keeps elaborating on. That same month his mother had gone off to the friend of her dead husband and the situation had just got too much. Berto had been in Class 1 of primary school and hadn't stood out in any way. After the accident he had begun to tell the most remarkable stories about his father, with whom he seemed to have conversations.

The most disturbing thing was that for a year he had been constantly crossing the street when the lights were red and apparently deliberately ran in front of passing cars. Conversations with his mother hadn't achieved anything – so he had come to the school for those with special needs. Apart from occasional fixed ideas and his fury whenever anything to do with 'dad' came up, things had gone much better with him.

Yesterday there was again a stir centred on Berto. He came to class late and was carrying a wooden crucifix about fifty centimetres tall under his anorak.

When I asked where he got it from, he quickly replied:

'From home; we've got lots of them. But this,' he added,' this isn't quite right.' He takes a red crayon and paints big red wounds on the wooden crucifix.

'Are you allowed to do that?'

'Yes, I've got to. When someone dies there's lots of blood.' He smears the body all over.

'That's enough,' I say and try to take it from him.

'No,' he protests, 'it's a present for Pedro, because he hasn't got a father either. So I've brought him God – even if sadly they killed him.'

He solemnly hands his dead God over to Pedro. Pedro receives this important gift equally earnestly and solemnly. He briefly holds the cross upright in front of him, then puts it in his arms – as one cradles a sleeping child. Both boys are serious and pay attention for the rest of the lesson. (Unfortunately there was a very tearful sequel, as the cross didn't come from home but from the school library.)

Berto is a child who was left alone as a result of the sudden and particularly gruesome accident which happened to his father. No one had spoken with him, nor had he been allowed to go to the funeral, so he had been left to himself. His father's death in an accident almost became an obsession. Because he was utterly alone, as a ghost his dead father became his constant companion.

The corner behind the waste-paper basket

Gert is very small and delicate for someone in Class 2. His big serious eyes are made even bigger by his spectacles and give him the expression of a intellectual little student. On the other hand his behaviour is far from being intellectual. He bangs the classroom door, throws down his school bag and slumps onto his chair, head on his arms. When I go on to tell a story he usually looks up and listens. Hope, longing, penetrating questions are in his gaze. I don't know his question – so how can we go in search of an answer?

And then the ritual which is always the same. His eyes suddenly go dark, his small lips are firmly pressed together, he gets up – and goes.

Simply goes out of the classroom, along the corridor, down the stairs. Sometimes I run after him, grab him, bring him back. He's there for another five or ten minutes, and then he goes off again.

But he's not the only one I have to teach. There are twelve pupils in this group. Sometimes it gets to me and I lock the classroom door on the inside. Nevertheless Gert suddenly disappears again. The door to the side room!

Gert is sitting on the floor in the corner. When he sees me he wants to run away. I hold him tight; he pants and kicks, but I'm stronger. I just hold him and sit with him on the floor. Suddenly his rigid little body goes soft and he begins to sob.

The other children come in. I send them back into the classroom. They are to paint. Gert has now rolled up in my lap like a kitten and weeps bitterly. I hear the others rampaging around next door. They would choose today to do it, I think – and stay sitting with Gert in my arms in the corner behind the wastepaper basket. He says a few words.

'Gert, I can't understand you.'

'Dad – dad – where's my dad . . .?'

'What's happened to your dad?'

'My dad . . . he's . . . he's in hospital . . .'

'Your dad is sick?'

'Yes, and auntie has said . . . because his heart . . . because for so long he's been . . . that, that . . . my dad . . .'

Gert can't go on.

'You're afraid that your dad will die?'

He gets up, stops crying and says loud and clear,

'Yes.'

Remarkably, he sounds almost relieved. We stand up, I take him by the hand and we go back to the others in the class. In this lesson, for the first time Gert paints a picture in his book like the other pupils.

The ritual of running away has now been replaced by another one. At the beginning of the lesson he comes up to me straight-away. I crouch down so that our eyes are at the same level and ask without further ado, 'How's your dad?' Then he usually answers equally directly, 'He's bad.' As he speaks, Gert drops his head forward, as if his neck were broken.

'And how are you?' I then ask.

'I'm afraid,' he says softly.

'You're afraid that your dad will die?'

'Yes,' he says, and looks at me.

'Now go and sit in your place,' I say without further ado; to an observer it might seem almost brutal. But Gert goes contentedly to his chair.

Since we've been beginning our lessons in this way, Gert has stopped running away and sometimes even joins in the lesson.

PS: Two weeks ago I had a great disappointment. Gert was not at the lesson. I asked his teacher about him. 'Gert has finally got a place at another special school.'

'Why's that?'

'You know, it's a school for children who are particularly difficult to teach. His running away got worse and worse. We couldn't take responsibility for him.'

Not dead – he hanged himself

Helga is a great dumpling of a girl. I'm a bit ashamed that I'm so totally unable to cope with her; she's far more difficult that a real scoundrel. Helga never causes a disruption, never says anything, and usually lies on the bench like a sleeping mountain.

On this particular day everyone comes to the lesson late. There's a representative of Alcoholics Anonymous in the school. They are clearly intrigued and we continue to talk about the topic. When Ramona states loudly, 'All drunken louts are bastards,' I try to formulate it more cautiously:

'They're often very sensitive people who have so tender a soul that they can't cope with a difficult, hard life.'

'Yes, Frau Hermann, that's right.' It's Helga. She's spoken for the first time this school year.

'You know, my dad is the dearest man. No one is as nice as he is, he lets you do anything, and he's also dished out money. My dad has never hit anyone, only mum, who keeps scolding and hitting me where she can. I wish she was dead instead of dad.'

'You dad is dead?'

'Not dead. He hanged himself, in the garden, last autumn. And I found him. The way he looked . . .'

Helga stares in front of her. All the pupils are silent, affected.

'And now without your dad are you very lonely?'

'No I'm not, I've four close friends.'

'Four, why four?

'If one hits me I take off and go to the next.'

Two weeks later Helga is absent.

'Is she sick?' I ask.

'A bit, you might say. Abortion, that's all.'

Whether it's true I don't know, nor do I bother to find out. It could be right, and that's the oppressive thing.

That was last school year. The distress of unsupported mourning for an obviously warm-hearted and generous father drives her into the arms of so-called 'close friends'. The fact that they now beat her suggests that she chooses friends who have drunk alcohol.

Reflections

'Children and Death', it says in the file which I've left in the staff room. 'Do you have to teach that kind of thing?' asks a colleague. 'That's a terrible subject! Quite perverse.' He shook his head as he said 'perverse'.

'Perverse' means 'wrong way round', something which just mustn't be allowed to happen. And when it nevertheless happens that death breaks into a child's life, we believe that we are protecting the children by keeping them from it: they are left alone with their questions and anxieties and with their often quite gruesome fantasies. Some children sense, feel quite clearly, that a dead person is not simply dead and gone, that such a person is near, and that it is up to us whether these experiences become a feeling of comforting companionship or a gruesome persecution. Repressed death becomes oppressive, and constrains life.

What can one tell a child about death? What we say is perhaps less important than that we should listen, listen to the questions, the ideas that a child has about death. A seriously ill twelve-year-old who says that he wishes that he had died in Dachau, where at least he could have talked about his fears, makes clear the distress of speechlessness.

If we leave death in its taboo corner, children's humanity is crippled. By contrast, their powers of hope are not cut off, but can develop, if we look at the experience of death with them. 'In the midst of life we are in death': death is part of life, the dark twin brother, but it doesn't make life poorer, paler. It is richer, more precious and colourful if we don't waste all our energies bracketing out death. I don't say all that, but I try to: always whenever the dark brother is in the class room. I don't chase him away but invite him to stay a while.

The experience of a bad death often meets up with the experiences of a bad life. Then abysses of sadness and fear of death open up, too deep and too dark to be brought to light afterwards and be written down. So the number of stories on this topic is particularly small. That contrasts with the observation that a disproportionate number of failed pupils are children who have experienced death or dying and have been left along with it. To put it simply: an experience of death in which there has been no support becomes an obstacle to learning.

Olli usually walks around bent, like someone who is carrying a rucksack that is far too heavy. Now I learn that his mother is in an alcoholic coma. If such a great and heavy 'stone' is put on top of all the everyday burdens of life, it's a miracle that such a child can still stand at all. On a walk in the hills it would never occur to us to expect a child to make any progress with such a burden, possibly uphill, and reach a specific destination. We would encourage the child to take off the rucksack, open it and, if he invited us, look in it together. What do you have at the bottom? So much. Do you need all that heavy stuff for your journey? Would you like to give me some of it? I can't take the whole rucksack from you or save you the journey, but first of all we can rest together. Look and sort, that's what support in mourning can seem like.

A hindrance to lamenting is a hindrance to life – and thus to learning. So we must make room for mourning.

Here we must realize that mourning often doesn't look 'mournful'. It is the most deeply hurt and older children in whom the course of mourning and a buried fear of death often turns on the surface into poisonous cynicism. Here it is just a matter of perceiving and sustaining. In this situation well-meant consolation or religious affirmations amount to a failure to observe the mourning and at best go into a void.

'The mystery of love is presence.' I know of nothing other than this sentence. And I also know that those who cannot hear because pain and anger close their ears can still feel, and are often particularly 'sharp of feeling'.

For a long time now, dying in our society has ceased to be an occasion for fellowship, as has mourning. In perceiving feelings, in allowing lament and accusation, in communication, we put dying, death and mourning back where they belong, in our midst.

Only recently it struck me that the words communication and communion are related. Can communication happen in such a way that we share the incomprehensible and in so doing experience that we human beings have two homes, here on earth and in the spiritual, the divine realm? Can the dark pit of our pain and mourning become a tunnel – a way through the darkness at the end of which I already see the way out, because it's getting lighter again? If together we recognize the growing brightness, that is the experience of the resurrection. I have hesitated to write this great word here, but I know of no other that will do better: if after the Good Friday event of death and despair, after the emptiness of the soul on Easter Saturday, if after that life becomes possible again, that is Easter. Thus the experience of dying and death can become the experience of our own immortal being.

That all sounds very fine, a colleague says. But perhaps it's a bit too optimistic. But can one do anything other than listen, endure, be there, perhaps do something practical? Yes, of course, and one should also keep crossing the boundary between education and pastoral care in the other direction.

It can be interesting to paint with all the children. Perhaps one tells us something in his or her picture, perhaps children succeed in steeping themselves through colours and symbols in a realm which words hardly reach. When children tell us their dreams or fantasy stories, sometimes we get a glimpse of the way in which they are grappling with dying. Looking together at the seasons and nature, the way things bud, blossom, mature, wither and then bud and grow again can give trust in a wise order. The transformation of cocoons into pupae, the development of a butterfly, is one of the best-known and most helpful images.

We owe a special treatment of the subject of death to a cold winter's day. Many of Class 5 were sick. The double lesson and the manageable group of nine children lured us into an outing. The woodland cemetery, the quiet morning of a winter day, the narrow paths between the graves in the snow, crosses and tombstones, heroes and angels, and then a colourful windmill on a child's grave – many questions, deciphering of inscriptions, serious conversation: what does being dead feel like? Suddenly cheerful shouting and in a flash a snowball fight is in full swing. 'Stop it, you must stop!' 'Why? Is it disturbing the dead?' 'No, but those who mourn.' After that it is only the great graveyard for soldiers from the world wars which really interests them: 'Every cross a dead person? Crazy, these wars.' I blow the whistle for our return. By now we've got completely frozen. We press into the warmth with the good smell of food. Everyone gets a hot bun; it tastes marvellous. When most have finished eating, I send them over to school. 'Bye till next week.' 'Is that the end? We haven't said the blessing yet,' moans Agron. 'Yes, but we haven't been in the classroom and here on the street . . .' 'There, behind the dustbin, that's a good place!' says Sylvia. We stand in a circle and it seems to me that I'm the only one who finds this a bit hard. Praying on the street? We say together, 'God bless us and protect us, make his face shine on us . . . Amen.' They run across to school. 'Where have you been in this cold?' asks a colleague who is coming their way. 'We've been visiting the dead, it was good,' says Daniel, and with enjoyment licks the bits of sugar from the corner of his mouth. 'Visiting the dead? Does that mean that you've been to the cemetery with the children? But they clearly enjoyed it.' My colleague is very perceptive. 'Children and death' is not perverse; quite the contrary, for childhood is a good time for such experiences: death in all its incomprehensibility is swallowed up in a precious, intensive life. They belong together.

5

Stupid Children, Wise Children

God's around me – even when the beer mugs fly

On my mantelpiece I find a letter, scrawled in pencil. 'Sorry I can't come tomorrow. Because my mum is marrying Rolf. Unfortunately. The baby's coming soon and she is terribly nervous and has half-throttled me again. Round the neck. I would like to come to RE but must go to the wedding. If I'm not at school I prefer to tell you. Your Irene.'

Around two weeks later. On Monday I have no school. About seven-thirty, still in my pyjamas, I'm enjoying a peaceful breakfast. There's a ring at the door. At this hour. Through the entryphone a thin voice: 'I must say something to you.'

'Irene! Has something happened?'

'Yes. No. But I want to tell you.'

'Come up and tell me what the matter is.'

Irene, from Class 6. A few weeks earlier she came to school with bad marks round her throat. When I ask about them she is almost making excuses. 'My mum, her belly keeps getting bigger and when the three little ones make so much noise she loses her nerve. Hitting the little ones gets her nowhere. After all, I am the oldest.'

'And what does hitting you achieve?' I asked her.

'Just that I help more.'

Rolf is the third 'dad' of the eleven-year-old.

Now she's standing at the door of my flat, so thin and small that she seems almost crippled by her big schoolbag. The anorak, with the sleeves rolled up, reaches almost to her knees. Only her glasses prevent her woollen hat from covering her whole face. The eyes behind the thick glasses seem even bigger, even bluer, today.

'Now Irene, what's happened?'

'He has surrounded me.'

She sounds quite simple, joyful and quiet at the same time.

'Surrounded? Who?'

'HE. "You surround me on all sides and hold your hand over me."'

'You mean our psalm. But I still don't understand . . .'

'God has surrounded me. It was like this. Mum and my new dad were fighting. And throwing things around. I was afraid and hid in my bed, under the cover. I could still hear them. Mum shrieked so. I thought that he was killing her. But I couldn't do anything . . .'

She breaks off and stares in front of her.

'And then?'

'Then at some point they went quiet. But I couldn't sleep. And I was frozen, although I still had my clothes on. But I was cold. And afraid. Then I still went to sleep. But only for a while. And then . . .' she smiled, 'then all at once HE surrounded me.'

'You felt God?'

She nodded.

'It was tremendously bright, and I didn't need to be afraid. Perhaps HE said it, I don't exactly know. But the fear simply went away. And then the brightness stopped. But it was still warm. And I went to sleep again. God surrounded me. Do you believe that too?'

She's quite certain, but looks at me questioningly.

'Yes, Irene, I believe that too.'

We're both quiet.

'When should you be at school?' it suddenly occurs to me.

'Not until the second lesson.'

'Have you had breakfast?'

She shakes her head: 'Since Rolf has been there I don't have breakfast. That's when mum is annoyed.'

'Take your anorak off and come over here.'

'But I've still got yesterday's clothes on. They're very badly crumpled.'

They're not only crumpled but also stink of beer: 'Because a bottle flew over into my corner which wasn't quite empty.'

I get a plate and a cup of milk.

'Come and sit down.'

'Do you always pray before eating?' Irene asks.

'Sometimes yes, sometimes no,' I reply truthfully.

'Would you like us to pray?'

'We could say our psalm together.'

We say together:

Lord, you search me out
and know me.
When I sit down or stand up you know it;
you understand my thoughts from afar.
Whether I walk or lie down, you are around me
and see all my ways.
For look, there is no word on my tongue,
that you, Lord, do not already know.
You surround me on all sides
and hold your hand over me.
This knowledge is too wonderful for me and too high,
I cannot understand it.

'Amen,' I say, 'now enjoy your food.'

She picks up the cup and puts it down again.

'Also the bit about the darkness.'

We go on:

Whither shall I go from your spirit?
And whither shall I flee from your face?
If I go to heaven, you are there;
if I lie down with the dead, look, you are there too.
If I were to take the wings of the dawn
and remain in the uttermost sea,
there too your hand would lead me
and your right hand would hold me.

If I said, 'Let darkness cover me
and night instead of light be around me,'
even darkness would not be dark with you
and the night would shine like the day.
Darkness is like the light.

She bites into her bread and honey with great pleasure, looks at me radiantly and says, 'I like your pyjamas, because they're so blue.'

'And I like your eyes, they're also very blue.'

For a while the two of us say nothing, devote all our attention to our bread and honey, surrounded inside and out with warmth and contentment. The sun moves to the right behind the television tower.

Irene gets up from her chair.

'It's 8.15 already. I must go, otherwise I'll be late.'

In the giant anorak she looks very small again.

'But don't tell anyone.'

'That you've come to see me?'

'No, that's no problem. But about my parents and about God. Otherwise they'll laugh at me.'

I look after her as she goes down the street in the early morning light. What a tiny little creature, and at the same time a human child who has experienced in night and fear that God surrounds her!

Odd, I'm not afraid now

The telephone rings. Jana. She has to go into hospital again for an examination.

'I'm so afraid I want to kill myself. I'm so afraid that I'd rather die.'

'What are you afraid of, Jana?'

'Of dying.'

'Of dying?'

'Yes, because perhaps I have a tumour, and if it grows . . . what do I do then? Can you help me?

'No, Jana, I can't help with a tumour.'

'Why not?'

'I can't.'

'But can I telephone you?'

'Yes, you can telephone me.'

'Any time, if I'm afraid?'

'Yes, any time, if you're afraid.'

'But I'm afraid almost every day. And sometimes, if I wake up, at night, too. Then it's worst.'

'You can telephone me then.'

'Do you hear the telephone at night?'

'Yes, I hear it at night, too.'

'Do you know? Shall I tell you something odd?'

'Tell me something odd.'

'Now I'm not afraid. At any rate, not now.'

I see because I don't see

'I only come for the stories. Because RE is really rubbish – that's what mum says, because God doesn't exist anyway,' announces Sven in a weighty tone.

'Why do we talk of God anyway, if we can't see him?' Karla wants to know.

I attempt to find an answer to this age-old question.

'Look, the air is all around us and in us and we don't see the air either, although . . .'

'But I see the air,' interrupts Pablo energetically.

'You see the air?'

'Yes, where I see nothing that's air. Where I see something, the cupboard or the table, that isn't air.'

'Is that what you think?'

'Pablo's making it up, seeing the air,' Sven sounds almost annoyed.

'But I do.' Pablo defends himself.

'I see the air because I don't see it, and because nothing, I mean nothing, that's not on. Is it?'

He looks at me in a questioning way.

'I simply can't imagine nothing.'

A statement made by Ernst Bloch. He probably would have enjoyed this little conversation partner.

I take up Pablo's idea.

'Nothing, that's not on, you said. And God, can it perhaps be something like that with God? He surrounds us even if we don't see him.'

'I should say,' says Jens feebly. Now he wants his story.

'We've forgotten our psalm,' Renate recalls. We say together.

Lord, you search me out and know me . . .
You surround me on all sides
and hold your hand over me.
This knowledge is too wonderful for me and too high,
I cannot understand it . . .

'But how can God have a hand if he's like the air?' For Karla the question isn't settled.

'An air-hand.' Sven is becoming impatient with the reflection on God that he has sparked off.

'Now, please, the story.'

'Yes, now I'll tell you a story . . . Pablo, why are you muttering to yourself?'

I don't want to admonish him; rather, I'm interested in every sentence that this often intimidated, sombre boy utters. He is hopelessly bad at writing and reading, but when he speaks it's often like a source of wisdom to which none of us has access.

'I was only saying . . . If only my father had an air-hand . . .' He goes red and lowers his head. I ask no more.

Two days later I meet Pablo on the stairs. It's a long time after the end of school.

'Don't you want to go home?'

'No . . .'

'That business about the air-hand – does you dad hit you, then?'

He nods.

'In the evening when he comes home?'

He doesn't come home in the evening. He's always at home. And when he's drunk . . . usually by lunchtime . . .'

'Should we go for a little walk together in the park?' I suggest. Earnestly and slowly he shakes his head.

'I've got to go home sometime. Otherwise my parents will worry.'

My cousin's child – a child of God

I've yet to fathom out Nina. Is she particularly stupid or perhaps very clever: smart, anyway? Anyway, she's very attractive: her dark complexion, shaggy black hair and amazingly voluptuous figure for a girl in Class 5. 'How old are you?' I ask her one day. 'I'll soon be thirteen,' she replies, and flounces away with coquettish triumph. That was last year.

In this new school year I've decided that she's stupid after all, at any rate yawning and uninterested. When she came to school, with heavy make-up, she simply flopped onto a bench and couldn't be motivated to put down her particularly beautiful writing on paper. Then she stayed away completely. I asked the class teacher. 'No point I worrying about truants,' she remarked.

Soon afterwards I met Nina in town. She came up to me quite happily. No, she just didn't want to go to school any more. Her parents? They couldn't care less; they hadn't spent long at school either. 'Don't you know,' she laughed proudly, 'we're gypsies.' 'Oh,' I remarked somewhat stupidly, and watched her sail off into the stream of passers-by like a ship, bedecked with chains, rings and bracelets.

A little later friends in the class say that Nina has a baby. Truly, a baby of her own! Very very tiny and jet black hair. That was some months ago.

Yesterday I met Nina shopping. I hardly recognized her. She is still attractive, but the bloom of youth has given way to the self-confident expression of a young woman. She puts a heavy bag on to the pushchair.

'Nina, hello!' I greet her. 'So it's really true that you have a child.' Now she blushes and is again more like the schoolgirl who will 'soon be thirteen'. 'That's what they always say. But this is my cousin's child,' she remarks defensively.

He's asleep. Little hands by his head. The image of wholeness and peace. 'What a specially beautiful child!' I say in warm admiration. 'Don't you think he's really specially beautiful?' 'Yes, quite specially beautiful. He looks so whole, protected. You know, "God bless and protect us . . ."?'

She nods. 'I've already said it to him.'

'The blessing? To the child?'

'Yes, once he was a bit sick, but only a bit. And now I must go home.'

'All the best to you both.'

Contentedly she goes off with the pushchair.

Is it really so important whether this child is hers or her cousin's? A child over whom Nina says the blessing when he is sick?

Mark can read. A proof of God?

Mark: 'What rubbish, resurrection. There isn't a God. Where is he then? Where is he? Where is he?'

I have to answer immediately. No time for theological reflection.

'In you. You're sometimes completely full of God, his power and wisdom, and when you tell us what you think about the world and people and animals you haven't thought it all up yourself. That's God in you. That's what I believe . . .'

His round mouth is wide open, and the aggression has suddenly gone.

'Yes, that's right!'

He pants deeply and loudly. Then, quite abruptly: 'Frau Hermann, may I read now?'

Mark reads. For the first time since I've been teaching him – in theory he can hardly read and write. But today he reads clearly and fluently in the consciousness that God's power is in him.

A month later. I daren't repeat the experiment. Can he still read? That would seem to me to be a misuse of the 'proof of God' given to both of us.

Why's the man laughing?

'Frau Hermann, have you ever seen a dead person? What do they look like? Disgusting, or sad, or evil? What do they look like?'

We're talking about dying. They want to know what kind of a feeling it is. I don't know precisely either. We reflect together. Susi tells what it was like when she wanted to take grandma her food and grandma didn't answer and was dead.

Marco tells how his brother died, and he wanted to see him, but the coffin was firmly closed.

The next day – I had thought very hard about this – I bring the photograph album *The Eternal Sleep* (faces of the dead photographed by R.Schäfer in the Charité Hospital). With great interest, almost devotion, they look at the faces of the dead: a child, an old woman, a young man, an old man. Many different people.

'They don't look at all sad.'

'Why is he laughing a bit?'

'It's as if she's having a beautiful dream.'

'Once again from the beginning, please, from the beginning again.'

We look at the pictures a second time. Then Melanie says:

'I know how it is. The soul is the inside of a person and the body is the outside.'

'Can you explain that to us?' I ask her.

Melanie: 'It's quite simple. First the soul is in the body and is glad because it's in it; then the soul can get out and is even more glad because now it has a lot of room. Perhaps that's why these are laughing.'

I noted down what Melanie said straight away, during the lesson. Melanie, small, pale and puny (perhaps the child of alcoholics?), who finds it very difficult to read and painful to write. But she clearly understands something about the soul.

Why do we have names?

'You look as if you've just climbed Everest,' comments a colleague in the staff room. And that's what I feel like.

It began quite innocently.

Anne and Sonia are now in confirmation class and wanted a bit of help with homework. 'Who invented baptism?' They have to ask their parents what they understand by baptism and why they had their children baptized. But if the parents haven't been baptized, then one can't expect much information from parents.

It's 24 June, a splendid day to talk about baptism. The climax of brightness and light in nature, the summer solstice; now the sun will be declining again, the light lessening, until in precisely six months we celebrate Christmas, the incarnation of the light of God, in the darkest and coldest time! They've listened amazingly attentively.

'But what has that to do with baptism?' is the legitimate question. I tell them about John the Baptist, whose birthday is celebrated on 24 June, and of the baptism of Jesus in the Jordan.

'He must increase, but I must decrease.' John baptized with water – Jesus with the Holy Spirit. And when we baptize a child today we also ask for the protection and power of the Holy Spirit.

'And what the Holy Spirit does – that is – I think . . . perhaps one can . . .'

'Don't you know precisely either?'

'You're right; I don't precisely know either in a way that I can put simply. Perhaps you can say that the Holy Spirit is near to God when we do something important.'

'So is the Holy Spirit also there when two people fuck?'

'Antonio, you pig!' squawks Renate. The others look at me expectantly.

'I think you're right. Antonio. When two people sleep together, that can have a very great deal to do with the nearness of God and the love of God.'

'Always?'

'I don't know. No, perhaps not always. Or . . . perhaps there is at least always the longing for God's love there.'

'I don't understand.'

'I believe you. But it's enough if you understand that God's love is also there when two people love each other.'

'When they make a child?'

'Yes, when a child comes into being, God's Spirit is certainly very near.'

'Then I'm almost baptized after all,' says Anne happily.

'How do you mean?' I ask in amazement.

'Because – my parents didn't have me baptized. I was baptized only after confirmation with Holy Spirit and so on. But then after all the Holy Spirit had already been with me when – I mean – what you said.'

'Because I said that the Holy Spirit is there when a child comes into being?'

'Yes. Then everyone has Holy Spirit in them whether or not they've been baptized. I think that's good.'

'It is, too, Anne.'

'And what happens to the Holy Spirit when I snuff it?'

Antonio again.

'Antonio, when you die, God's Holy Spirit is quite certainly in you.'

'Quite certainly?'

'Yes, I believe, quite certainly.'

How can I talk about this unplanned 'ascent of Mount Everest'? Who can bear the clumsy, often obscene, language of the children and at the same time understand the breadth and depth of their questions? The extent of their experience of suffering transcends that of many adults – rarely has it dulled them but made them more impatient with adults, sometimes brutal, often cheeky. Courtesy and conformism are not values for them, and that makes it often so difficult for us who have been socialized in a middle-class way to deal with them. Have their environment, their parents, their neighbours ever been 'courteous', friendly and relaxed towards them? And 'conformist?' Haven't they been terrifyingly assimilated to a society in which they experience impatience leading to a lack of concern and a striving to make money which extends to a lack of scruples?

I'm still sitting at the desk. Shall I go on with 'baptism' in the next lesson or do 'guilt and forgiveness', which is prescribed in the syllabus?

The baptism insertion today was exhausting enough.

That evening I go to a lecture. It's after ten when I catch my tram. Loud shouting, mixed with the cries of children: a mob of young people are pushing, kicking and fighting at the tram stop. They could be my pupils, I think. Then I recognize Antonio in the midst of them! Hitting around him on the ground like a lunatic and shrieking with his still high voice. 'Antonio,' I call, this time louder, and push between them. Some are so amazed that the tumult suddenly stops. 'What in the world are you doing here at this time?' I ask in a schoolmistress's tone.

'Me, nothing. Playing.' He has got up and wipes the blood off his nose with his hand. He looks quite content. He's obviously had a splendidly amusing time.

'Is he yours? Damned cheeky for someone his age,' says a grown-up.

'I know. Come on, get on the tram!' I tell Antonio.

He sits opposite me, neither weary nor exhausted.

'Why did you call out my name so loudly?' he wants to know.

'So you could hear me. That's what names are for.'

Next RE lesson.

By now Anne and Sonia have had their confirmation classes. In them they sit with grammar-school children who are also one or two classes above them and they certainly feel sometimes that it's all too much. That makes it all the more welcome that they bring questions with them to school – this school which they quite evidently also feel to be protection, where they can have trust, even if they are far from being 'model' pupils. 'Why do children get their names at baptism?' they want to know today.

'It isn't quite like that. Even children who aren't baptized have names, but the pastor mentions the name of the child when he has said "I baptize you in the name of the Father and the Son and the Holy Spirit."'

'God calls people by name. Whenever we say a person's name, there's a bit of God's call there,' I try to explain.

Enough talking. We write in the book:
'God says, I have called you by your name, you are mine.'
Antonio pipes up.
'Is that why you called me by my name yesterday?'
'Because of what?'
'So that I wouldn't fight – because of God and all that.'
'Yes. Perhaps you're right. I want to you to remain intact. You're certainly one of Satan's brood, but you're also a child of God.'

Antonio beams. He can recognize himself in these extremes.

Two weeks later he's absent – for a whole month. He's in hospital with a complicated fracture of the nose. I send him a little packet and get a card from him in very bad spelling: 'Thanks for the sweets. They're OK. Your Antonio.'

My Antonio.

He is one of seven children. Already, at eleven, he's completely neglected. When I asked him what his parents said when he only got home at eleven o'clock at night he shrugged his shoulders. 'Couldn't care less. Usually they don't even notice. If they do, I get beaten. But that doesn't matter.'

Despite everything, this rascal exudes so much power and cheerfulness: he's like his splendid pictures – colourful, wild and exotically beautiful. How middle-class parents would nurse and encourage these talents! But Antonio is already neglected, wicked, bubbling over. He will grow up to come into conflict with many limits and laws – and with all his unruliness perhaps not grow old at all. Yet a joy in life bubbles from every pore. And I am convinced that God has called him by his name.

Nietzsche and Rilke – but not with these pupils

Having been good for two years at joining in blessings and prayers, they suddenly don't want any more of it. 'Now we're too old for that!' remarked a girl, and a boy added that he too didn't feel at all 'protected'.

What am I to do? Force the prayers and blessing on them, despite their resistance, or remove them without providing a sub-

stitute? Perhaps they're even right. In Class 8 of a mixed-ability
school pupils aren't usually fourteen but rather fifteen or sixteen,
an age at which they enjoy putting critical questions. So I had the
bright idea of telling them about a boy called Friedrich who lost
his father at an early age, and was first brought up by three
bigoted women and then in a monastically strict boarding
school. At the age of twelve he said that the Trinity consisted of
God the Father, God the Son and God the Devil, and at the end
of his schooldays could no longer cope with the God who had
been preached to him for nineteen years. What interested him
was the 'unknown God'. I was amazed how interested the pupils
became in this violent, gifted boy who fled with his poems from
the darkness of the cold damp walls of Schulpforta. When I
brought Nietzsche's poem 'To the Unknown God' to the next
lesson, they were quite ready to learn it and say it at the beginning of the lesson instead of a 'proper prayer'.

> Once again, before I go onwards
> and send my gaze forwards,
> in solitude I lift my hands
> to you to whom I fly,
> to whom in the deepest depths of my heart
> I solemnly dedicated altars,
> so that all the time
> my voice calls you again.
>
> On them glows deeply inscribed
> the words 'To the unknown God'.
> I am his, even if I have remained
> to this hour in the wicked herd . . .
> I am his – and I feel the snares
> that pull me down in battle
> and – though I flee,
> I still commit myself to his service.
>
> I want to know you, unknown one,
> you who grasp deep into my soul,
> sweeping through my life like a storm,

incomprehensible, akin to me.
I want to know you, to serve you.

It doesn't matter here whether every word, every sentence is understood. It is the homelessness, the thrust of the search which they pick up and in which they rediscover themselves.

I first of all doubted whether I was justified in replacing the God of the Bible with the unknown God at the end of school. Then I thought of Paul on the Areopagus. He too took up the unknown God, in order to speak with the Athenians of the living God: 'What therefore you worship as unknown, this I proclaim to you. . . They (people) should seek God, in the hope that they might feel after him and find him. Yet he is not far from each one of us' (Acts 17.22, 27). So I feel in good company, with Paul and the children, in detecting Christ, 'the Lord of those without religion', on ever new ways.

One pupil of this Class 8 deserves special mention. Bernd, perhaps stimulated by the story of the young Friedrich Nietzsche, picked up in the flea market what he called a 'book of poems', the complete poems of Catullus in Latin and German. Now, in the steps of Catullus, he is himself writing poetry, some of it gripping yet clumsy love poetry, but also poems of fear and hope.

Anyone who has seen the look with which he hands over one of his poems, something like sly bliss, can hardly believe that Bernd is otherwise a particularly difficult pupil – neglect, theft. Even if in the not so distant future Bernd should land in jail – 'the wicked herd' – he has tasted the happiness of searching and perhaps in it sensed something of this unknown, incomprehensible figure who is related to him.

Classifications like 'stupid' and 'shrewd' become irrelevant. That is the case when someone from Class 7 notes that human beings are 'baked together like God and the devil'. Only a human being can be utterly good and very bad at the same time. Do I give this boy an E, because he can never learn a psalm by heart, read a saying without making a mistake, or do I give him an A, the very best of As, because he can put such a deep truth into words almost as a matter of course?

Here is a further example to clarify this special wisdom which bursts the framework of any skill.

One day just before spring, when the new shoots in nature seemed to be extending to the unruly bodies of the pupils, I went out with them into the park. I wanted to pick that up in the next lesson and wrote on the board a poem by Rilke:

Hardness disappeared, and all at once
new growth opened up on the drab meadow,
little streams change the emphasis.
Tendernesses reach from space
down to the earth.
Ways go far into the land and show it,
unsuspecting you see an expression of its rise
in the empty tree.

Playing the teacher, I ask them what it reminds them of. Nothing. Last week? No, we were in the park. They aren't the brightest, I think and attempt to help them with a paraphrase. When the days get brighter, heaven reaches down to earth, and at the same time sap and power rise above when heaven and earth combine so that new things can grow. What time is it? 'Why didn't you say that straight away? RE lesson of course.' Now I'm the one who finds it hard to understand: 'RE lesson? What do you mean?' 'When you talk about God and those holy things, that's the power from above, and we, I mean, I and the others, we're the power from below. And that comes together in RE.' I'm flabbergasted. 'And then something new can come into being?' 'I think so,' he comments calmly.

RE teaching like the prelude to spring: the powers of heaven and earth combine for something new to grow – has there ever been a better definition? That day I leave school ennobled, ennobled by a pupil with learning difficulties.

Reflections

'Believe in God, no. If you could see him, but? No one has ever seen him, or have they?' We consider this together. Would we recognize him? What would he look like? The Israelites made themselves a golden calf when their longing for the visible God became too great. God a calf? No, better not that. Our perplexity has got to all of us.

Two weeks to Christmas, the birth of Christ, the boy Jesus, the child, the man in whom God's Spirit . . . 'Ah,' interrupts Roberto and taps his forehead, 'now I see it: Christmas is to remind us that there was God was always there to lend a hand.' Is that a stupid insight?

A God to lend a hand and a God to intervene in the life of these often so desperate children! How often I've wished that he were here. Not the grasping, the radiant God in the heights – we must seek him in the depths, the God who dwells in darkness. As Rilke put it: 'People always look away from God. They seek him in the light . . . above. And God dwells elsewhere – waits – right at the ground of everything, where the roots are.'

Thing are usually pitiful even around the 'roots' of these children. Where is the basis of trust and reliability in which they could flourish? Instead of roots which further growth we can often recognize excessive signs of damage, of the kind that we see in sick trees. A twelve-year-old who says, 'When I think of the future – I'd rather not think', has his future poisoned.

For fear of what is coming to me, I would prefer not to think. Fear of my father's unemployment, of my parents' divorce, of wars, fear of the pollution of the environment: food, drinking water, air, all that is poisoned anyway. You get skin cancer from the sun, says mother. You get Aids from love, says father. By the time I'm grown-up I've had it anyway, says the child. People used to be able to exploit the earth, say the youth, all we're left with is a rubbish dump.

'Should I be my brother's keeper?' This question, handed down from the beginnings of the history of humankind, seems today to have found its pernicious continuation: 'Should we be our children's guardians?' I may not and cannot protect not only the present life of my brother but also the future basis of the life of our children. And they sense that. So their inner loss of a future leads to a devaluation of the present and thus often to giving themselves up. This is a psychological process which Viktor Frankl observed in concentration camps and which takes an almost terrifyingly similar course in these children. They are so afraid of the future that they cannot learn, can hardly summon up any interest in anything. 'Fear makes people stupid' – an observation which has often been attested.

What a good thing it is that RE isn't a typical discipline! To begin with I believed that research into causes could be helpful against fear, but I've become increasingly dissuaded of that. Where fear and despair are expressed, they are allowed to exist, and I perceive them. But I've learned to distinguish between the garage to which I take my car to be mended when it breaks down and my RE lessons. Here I trust my teaching far less: I can't simply repair what has broken down in the soul, nor can I change the soul for a new one.

While I'm writing this sentence, the door bell rings. Lena is standing in front of me. I don't recognize her immediately. She left two years ago without taking the leaving exam. 'Don't you recognize me any more?' She sounds shocked. 'Come over here and let's have a look at you,' I say – although I don't like being disturbed like this. Now I recognize her again, the very blue, sad eyes and the narrow face. 'Of course I recognize you now.' An almost relieved smile slips over her pale face. 'Do you remember that time, the business with my father . . . And then I went into a home.' I remember that too. Lena tells how she tried to catch up and do the leaving exam, but then she had to go into the clinic again. The clinic? 'Yes, I'd tried to commit suicide a second time. I'm simply afraid. Always afraid. They all say I've a chance. But I can't believe it. What for? Life is so shitty. It's not worth it. What do I need a leaving certificate for?' Should I tell her that that life isn't just shitty, that a leaving certificate may perhaps be worth while and that her fears of everything are unfounded? Can I instil courage for the future into her, by talking her out of her fear for the future? We eat dates and drink tea. When it gets dark I light two candles and put the vase in the candlelight. 'Do you always have roses?' 'Not always.' 'I love roses.' So do I. Would you like another date?' 'They taste really good.' 'I think so too.'

We don't have a deep conversation or exchange any lofty thoughts. She is too sad and I am too helpless. Yet something changes, we feel peace and warmth, at least for this hour. When she goes, she asks, 'Can you give me your telephone number again . . .' I give it to her. 'Would you like my number too? It's my birthday on 11 March, in case you wanted to telephone.'

Her telephone number is here with the dialling code on my paper, and now I shall copy it into my diary. It isn't as if Lena came at that precise moment to emphasize the sentence which I had just written; and my remark that I can't 'repair anything'. But didn't she tell me her birthday? The day on which she began her life. All at once it was important enough to mention it. After telling me about the days on which she only wanted to die, she tells me the day on which she was born 'in case' I want to telephone. Is it an invitation to keep the bow of loving

perception taut, not to forget again her, her fear of life, her hopelessness?

If I can manage this . . . I catch myself hoping that she could also pass
her final examination. Erich Fromm speaks of 'productive love'. Love
against fear? Does that mean love against stupidity?

6

Conclusion

The boy who some years ago said, 'I'll probably become a criminal', is now in a young offenders' prison. I was able to go and see him; we were loosely in contact even after his expulsion from school. So my RE was no use? Yes. It was no use, but it did change something. Two people have met, they've sometimes talked of God and also argued about him, and in this struggle they've found love and warmth for each other. Isn't that something?

By what do I measure the success of an RE course? By knowledge of the Bible, by the taking of leaving exams, by settling down in life?

When a school chaplain says that RE teachers are 'the mine dogs of the church, far outside it, going where the church has long since failed to reach', he is saying two things. Here teachers are appointed where it can easily be seen that in terms of church statistics it is hardly worth while; where they work is simply too far outside, remote from any belonging to a middle-class society. Secondly, these teachers – like any capable mine dog – are running a high risk of being hurt, in their faith, in their self-esteem, their hopes for the future. For RE teachers there is no guarantee of being edifying or coming out with soul intact.

Nevertheless, it is the sparks of light in the night which can make us more certain of the light than bright daylight.

Along comes this little mistrustful Benno, ready to hit or to kick. 'Do you want to see my collection of monsters?', and before I have brushed him off, a considerable number of cards with grisly faces have been laid out on the table. 'You can choose one for yourself.' When I say that I don't actually need a monster, he says understandingly: 'Because you're more interested in God and that sort of thing. But I don't have a picture of that. You can take the monster that you think is most beautiful.' I finally choose a greenish-brown one with a scarred face from which a bird of prey is growing; its hands are claws, and the sky behind it is streaked with lightning. For many days it lies on my desk. Benno, this brutal little chap whom I could hardly bear, becomes more important to me every day. For the next lesson I bring him a little angel card as a present. Contentedly he puts it with his collection of monsters. 'Now we've each given the other something,' he says, and looks at me like a friend. Sparks of light in the dark.

A girl has read on a car sticker, 'Jesus is coming'. She wants to know whether I believe that. I don't know. 'What do you believe he would do if he really came?', she asks. 'I don't know,' says my mouth once again, but my heart knows that he would come here into the classroom, to these children first. And then I tell myself that many others ask if these children are worth it!

Their fates, their laments, their accusations against life express the deepest human longing for God. Can I make them feel that this longing for wholeness is at the same time a reflection of God's longing for people? Not only do we seek God, for example in RE, but he also seeks us – for example in RE.

If Antonio – that is my name for the boy who had the age of twelve was already convinced that he would become a criminal – if Antonio has understood with his heart that God is looking for him, is interested in him, even when he has done bad things and is in the youth detention centre, then he has understood the most important statement in salvation history.

There are other good grounds for the activity of the 'mine dogs' in this apparently hopeless terrain. When a class teacher who says that she has no time for religion regrets that her children no longer have RE, my ears prick up. She can't cope with all the desperation, hurt and fear that is unloaded in aggression during a lesson which is meant to be teaching something. 'These children are really ruined. We need a school psychologist, but as we don't have one, RE also does a lot.' She has noticed that the children who have RE twice a week, in which notice is taken of their difficulties and problems without the stress of learning, clearly become more relaxed and generally peaceful. I don't mind being regarded as a kind of substitute school psychologist. After all, isn't pastoral care the most basic task of the church? 'Attentive hearing is a form of love,' Romano Guardini once remarked.

And is it really crazy to read Rilke with little thugs, to learn Nietzsche off by heart with the neglected, and to discuss the life and work of Stephen Hawking, perhaps the most brilliant, severely handicapped scientist of our time, with those who have learning difficulties? Almost always they grasp respect for the greatness and dignity of human beings that is intended by God, and is independent of gifts and social status, recognize the human being in every garb and mutilation. One becomes aware that one cannot have a vague feeling of compassion or affection at the latest when the children get out of hand, often in a cruel way. 'Goodness must have a sharp side, otherwise it is confused with stupidity.' I have written this remark by Albert Schweitzer on the cover of some preparation notebooks. And so RE can become a sometimes quite inconvenient form of self-knowledge and self-education.

'Child violence is inseparable from adult violence,' I wrote down somewhere, and thought how good it was that I myself wasn't violent. That is, until I was taught better – or rather worse. My loud shouts couldn't stop Rocco chasing little, intimidated Nathalie (she's only recently come to Germany, and lives with her aunt after both her parents had been killed before her eyes). I run down the corridor after them. Too late. Nathalie has crouched under a line of coathooks; she's trapped. Rocco kicks out with his heavy winter boots and hits her in her fear-filled face. I tear him away and hit him on the ear. My dismay was great, not so much because of Rocco's pain or about this breach of school rules but because I had found myself using uncontrolled violence. I had gone off the rails, lost it; I had been neither controlled nor loving, and had hit a child in a quite ordinary way, out of rage and impotence.

This bad blow set off an amazing process. When I began to teach some years ago, these schools were still called 'special schools'. For me the term 'special school' indicated something that was exceptional, set aside, even cut off. I increasingly asked myself whether their world was not perhaps the more normal one: an everyday life to which the experience of unemployment, alcoholism and sexual abuse belonged as naturally as music lessons and riding holidays in middle-class families. For me the way to these children – including the way of talking to them – seemed infinitely long. Would I ever reach them? When in the first months I stumbled from being at my wits' end to despair, and from despair to helplessness, precisely this became the way to them. It is not so bad for them to find me helpless and imperfect as long as I remain authentic. They do not need the perfect teacher, but the person who does not turn away from their imperfections, from the cruelty and obscenity, in order to work with clean shoes in a cloudcuckoo land. For the first time I began to understand Paul (II Corinthians 12ff.). God replied to him: 'Let my grace be enough for you, for my strength has its power in weakness . . . Therefore I am of good courage in my weakness. For when I am weak, I am strong.' And shouldn't that apply to us RE teachers too?

For these children all that matters is what we are, not what we present. Being imperfect, weak, nervous, unjust, they forgive all that without further ado, as long as we are truthful. When a pupil asks, 'Pray for me every day until I get back from hospital,' I can say 'Yes' only if I really do it and am prepared to concede – they almost always ask – that sometimes I was too lazy or too tired.

There are times when the very thought of the effort of teaching becomes too much for me and I dread the next lesson. If I go to my pupils with this attitude I'm lost. Or more precisely, we are lost because we can only feel the annoyance in one another. When I noticed that it was very much worse the more I put the children, particularly the bad ones, out of my mind during the days between the RE lessons, I tried the opposite. I imagined them to myself. Very soon I would picture them, usually their

faces, in a relaxed moment. When I then met them a week, or
three or four days, later, there was a sense of warmth or relax-
ation: friendliness rather than alienation.

I write this down here because it is so unbelievably helpful and
effective. The time it takes to keep each child – it needn't be all
the classes at once – briefly in this inner light is richly com-
pensated for by a quite different possibility of encounter, even
with the most difficult pupils, indeed particularly with them.

The one who loves intensive life, a place where nothing can
become routine, where life and learning belongs together like
light and shadow, is right here. Together we experience that
there is no whole world, but there is much wholeness in the
world, and it is worth tracking it down.

Luise Rinser, herself a teacher, describes the experience that
only a constantly renewed power of love can provide a way out
of despair and helplessness in teaching:

> I was completely desperate . . . The step . . . into real school life
> becomes possible only if one throws all the methods one has
> learned overboard and wants to see nothing but the child as
> someone who is learning . . . I am inclined to see the whole
> business of being a teacher as simply inculcating into the
> children the one feeling that I love them and that in this love
> they experience that despite the wretchedness, the sorrow, the
> spiritual hunger, there is something else which means power.
> We call it spirit; in practice I call it love.

So do I.